CAB LOG

http://ulpress.org
University of Louisiana at Lafayette Press
P.O. Box 43558
Lafayette, LA 70504-3558

Printed on acid-free paper in the United States
Library of Congress Cataloging-in-Publication Data

Names: Legg, Dege, author.
Title: Cablog : diary of a cabdriver / Dege Legg.
Description: Lafayette : University of Louisiana at Lafayette Press, 2020.
Identifiers: LCCN 2020032214 | ISBN 9781946160706 (paperback)
Subjects: LCSH: Legg, Dege. | Taxicab
   drivers--Louisiana--Lafayette--Anecdotes.
Classification: LCC ML420.L298 A3 2020 | DDC 781.62/410763092 [B]--dc23
LC record available at https://lccn.loc.gov/2020032214

Cover design by Megan Barra

CAB LOG

DIARY OF A CABDRIVER

DEGE LEGG

University of Louisiana at Lafayette Press
2020

To all the dreamers out there,
working tough jobs and trying to make sense of it all.

Much thx, Susie!
x

TABLE OF CONTENTS

CHAPTER 1
MOTEL CITY

CHAPTER 2
TRAILERVILLE

CHAPTER 3
THE GRIND

CHAPTER 4
NOWHERESVILLE

FOREWORD
by Scott Jordan

In mid-'90s New Orleans, the bar Checkpoint Charlie wasn't for the faint of heart, especially after midnight. Lurking on the edge of the French Quarter, Checkpoint doubled as a laundromat, late-night eatery, and pool joint. Its clientele was a mix of bikers, goths, barflies, tourists, and service industry refugees, and Charles Bukowski would have felt right at home in the permanent cigarette haze and noxious urine-and-vomit puddles lurking right outside Checkpoint's doors.

That's where I first encountered Dege Legg.

Dege (pronounced "Deej") was thrashing away with his band Santeria. Checkpoint's unforgiving atmosphere made it fertile ground for veteran bluesmen and young punk rockers, with Santeria firmly in the latter camp. Hailing from Lafayette, Louisiana, Dege's crew wasn't trafficking in regional zydeco chank-a-chank or Cajun waltzes. This was unapologetic, in-your-face, guitar-driven chaos, with a murky, hypnotic undercurrent fitting its namesake. Dege was its front man and visionary.

I was suitably impressed and pegged Santeria as a Louisiana band-to-watch in national music-biz broadsheet *Billboard* magazine. That sparked some correspondence with Dege, and I kept tabs on him while writing for New Orleans's *OffBeat* magazine and *Gambit Weekly*. Santeria eventually broke up a decade or so later, but Dege soldiered on with similarly intriguing projects. When he founded Black Bayou Construkt, he proudly emblazoned the band's logo on its touring van and painted it, of course, black. Nothing brightened my day more than seeing Dege rumbling around in this nocturnal warhorse straight out of *Mad Max*.

The apocalyptic, mystical strain running through Dege's music is no act. When I moved to Lafayette in 2003 to edit and write for the *Independent Weekly*, we talked and visited more frequently—and at times I feared for his safety. With his guerilla DIY ethos hatched as an '80s kid building illegal skate ramps and devouring fringe zines, Dege hatched one gonzo project after another. He lived in and filmed music videos in the seediest motel in town. Commandeered remote cornfields and obsessed over crop circles. Documented his fixation with UFOs. Jerry-rigged a dobro with fireworks. To say he lived life firmly on the edge would be an understatement.

That's why I was highly skeptical when a colleague told me that Dege wanted to talk to me about a job opening at the newspaper. It was for a calendar coordinator and arts and entertainment writer, the unglamorous position of compiling nightclub listings and pitching story ideas in hopes of earning writing clips. I couldn't wrap my brain around him working in an *office*. I quasi-interviewed him for the position, essentially asking, "Are you sure you want to do this?"

Dege had been driving a taxi at night for steady-ish income. Lafayette, despite its charms and having been named the Happiest City in America, has some dark corners. Grinding poverty and shaky public education snake their way through side roads and surrounding towns. Dege, true to form, was regularly finding himself behind the wheel for unimaginable scenarios with unimaginable customers in unimaginable locations. The dystopian strangeness of some of his fares compelled him to keep a diary/journal/cablog.

Like many dedicated songwriters (see: Springsteen, Bruce; Cash, Rosanne; Morrissey, Bill), it turns out that Dege is a talented writer, period. Excerpts from his cablog was one of the first projects we worked on together after he earned the gig at the *Ind*, and he went on to publish numerous memorable pieces, especially a cover story for which he embedded himself in numerous homeless camps on the hidden side of Lafayette's train tracks. Dege's prose and interests reflect the man himself: gritty, honest, unflinching, questioning, and empathetic.

Our newspaper days are long behind us, and Dege is currently known worldwide as Brother Dege, thanks to the inclusion of his song "Too Young to Die" in Quentin Tarantino's *Django Unchained*. A quarter century after our first encounter at that squalid Checkpoint show, Dege now sounds like a bona fide Delta bluesman, stomping his heel and howling out his original chronicles of pain and restlessness, armed with his wandering spirit and a Resonator guitar.

Cablog is an arresting chapter in Dege Legg's artistic journey, and I'm thrilled that UL Press is giving it the rich treatment it deserves.

Welcome to riding with Dege. Strap in.

Scott Jordan has covered Louisiana music and arts for three decades. His work has appeared in The Rolling Stone Jazz and Blues Album Guide, Downbeat, *the* Austin Chronicle, The B.B. King Companion, *and numerous other publications. He's also written liner notes for releases from artists ranging from Johnny Sansone to Stevie Ray Vaughan. He teaches English at the Episcopal School of Acadiana in Cade, Louisiana.*

ACKNOWLEDGMENTS

Much thanks to Steve May, Cherry Fisher May, Odie Terry, and Scott Jordan of the *Independent Weekly* in Lafayette, Louisiana, for kicking off my taxi-writing experiment by publishing my initial article on the subject ("Meter Man," *The Independent Weekly*, No. 41, June 23, 2004). Additional thanks to Margaret A. Harrell, Michelle Martin Clark, and R. Reese Fuller for their help in the editorial process.

And lastly, thanks to all of the people out there who have been so kind in supporting my writing pursuits over the years.

INTRODUCTION

Every job is its own adventure. Driving a cab on the night shift in Lafayette, Louisiana, from 2003 to 2008 was no different. There were inspiring highs, crushing lows, moments of terror, hilarity, nonsensical absurdity, and endless nights of banal routine punctuated with moving episodes that would quietly restore one's faith in humanity. It was a wild run.

The entries in this book are true stories culled from those years in chronological order beginning with my rookie year to my final year of employment at the cab company—roughly five years total. The first year was an exhilarating run through the dark underbelly of the city—the drunks, druggies, the nightlife, the prostitutes, and the regular folks. The middle years were a period wherein much of the chaos of the job became somewhat routine. My fifth and final year could be described as an exhausting stage of burnout. The dramatic highs and lows of the job began exacting an emotional and experiential toll that caused me to often loath the job, the clientele, myself, and ultimately my deeper motivations for remaining in this line of work.

Yes, each job was its own adventure; each job was also its own book, depending on the amount of time and emotion invested in it. In this case, aside from short-term financial subsistence, I was not so invested in taxi driving as a career, but as an experience that, if captivating enough, I could also document in writing. A great deal of emotional energy was forged into those special moments and shared experiences with the passengers. And as my time at the job progressed, I realized this CABLOG document was not so much about *me* as a protagonist, but about *them* and my reactions to them.

As the book moves forward, the details of my personal life disappear into the experiences of passengers. I function more like a warped lens through which the reader absorbs each interaction, while possibly digesting some of some idiosyncrasies, defects, and advantages of its construction.

That was my job, and this is my book.

Enjoy the ride.

Chapter 1
MOTEL CITY

MOTEL CITY

This is the end of the line. I'm living in a cheap motel in Lafayette, Louisiana. Room #109. $165/week. I've got $81 in my pocket and no job. Most of the residents are tenured alcoholics. They drink cheap beer, meander around the parking lot, and blow smoke into the hole where expectations go to die as the cable TV flutters and the passing traffic growls.

There is nothing to do here but poke through the rubble of dead dreams. It is here in these motels that capitalism crashes into the sad reality of losers on the ragged journey to rock bottom. It's the last stop before homelessness, one hundred yards from the train tracks. It is here that your dinner drops from a coin-fed vending machine. It is here that America comes to die or to hide from the inevitable.

This place is like an abandoned carnival ride half-buried in the sand. It's all here, leaning into the clock and slipping away. Nobody cares. Or pretends to care. They just exist and survive, as prostitutes swat flies and junkies wander the sun-bleached concrete and ex-carnies belch behind the Molotov drapes and dig through the archeological trash of a past life, waving at ghosts, puffing on cheap cigarettes and cheaper beer.

As the MileWideSun
Pounds down upon us.
It's merciless
And inescapable for now.

A week ago, I was living in a three-bedroom house with a front yard and a dog and a dishwashing machine. Today, I'm in this crap motel. Alone and nearly broke. But strangely enough, I am freer than I've ever been, because I've already lost this leg of the race.

And the fall is not that far.
It's like a truce in a war with everyone.
I'm not happy.
I'm not sad.
I'm just stuck here.
Waiting.
In a holding pattern.
I stare out of the window

With my fists clenched around the burglar bars
And dream
And wonder what comes next.

I'm alive as any of them and no deader than the rest. There are no expectations here. All promises have been broken like long shot prayers in the slaughterhouse of love. Before the blade comes down.

No one comes here to be remembered.

They come here to forget.

And be forgotten.

I NEED A DAMN JOB

In order to avoid going any lower on the sacred ladder of success, I have to get a job. And survive. Buy food. Pay rent. And do whatever else is expected of me in this life. I have a college degree. But a degree in philosophy in the Deep South doesn't get you shit. It's like a degree in astrology or bird-watching or balloon animals. Nobody cares. It's worse than being a musician, which is my other job that doesn't pay well.

All I need right now is a shit job and a regular paycheck, so that I'm not dead weight on this runaway train also known as the current state of my life. So, I open the newspaper and scan the classified ads.

JOBS AVAILABLE
Dishwashers
Pipefitters
Truck drivers
Laundry workers
Sanitation workers
Must have a clean driving record
No felons
Must have transportation
Much pass drug test
Good attitude

These jobs are all shit. Or varying degrees of shit. Of the hundreds of classified ads, only one seems even slightly appealing:

WANTED: CAB DRIVERS
Good Pay. Good driving record.
Must be 21 or over and have Chauffeur's permit.
Apply in Person.

Could be interesting.

Later that day, I drive to the address listed in the ad, which, strangely enough, is not far from the wasteland of my motel. The cab company is located in an industrial park in a run-down section of town. It's a giant tin building, wreathed in weeds and barbed wire. In a gravel side lot, there is a field of cabs. Some are in working condition. Some not.

I enter the building. Two guys sit at a table and sip coffee.

Who do I talk to about applying for a job?

"You want to drive or dispatch?"

Drive.

He points down a hallway. I walk in that direction. Look around. Pass a storage closet and a day room where drivers sit and wait to start their shifts. I keep walking and approach an office. Sitting inside is a man. Salt-and-pepper hair. Late fifties. Tall.

Is this where I apply to be a driver?

"Come in. Sit down."

His name is Joe. He will later tell me he is from Palestine but grew up in Kuwait. Most of his family lives in Jordan. He eventually migrated to the U.S. to attend college in Louisiana. He is the boss. He's friendly and relaxed.

"How's your driving record?"

Good.

"Are you a convicted sex offender?"

Nope.

"Do you have any DUIs?"

No.

"Can you work nights?"

Yes.

"Are you good with people?"

Most of the time.

"Are you on drugs?"

No.

"Can you start on Friday?"

Yes, I can.

"You're hired."

He quickly explains to me the process of getting a chauffeur's permit. You need a permit to get the job. You also need a Class D license. This requires another driving test at the DMV.

"Bring them with you on Friday. We'll do the paperwork then."

OK. Thanks.

I exit and drive back to the motel.

I can't believe it. I got a fucking job.

4

HERE'S THE DEAL

The taxi cabs stay on the road twenty-four hours a day, 365 days a year. They never stop. Drivers work in twelve-hour shifts, 4 a.m. to 4 p.m. or the opposite. I am assigned to the night shift. So, I will work from 4 p.m. to 4 a.m. There is no hourly wage. Each driver makes 45-percent commission on the shift's fares. If you bring in a hundred dollars, you take home forty-five.

The days all start the same. Show up at the cabstand between 3 and 4 p.m. Sign in on the sheet. Wait to get assigned a cab. Eventually, someone calls your name and hands you the keys to a cab for that particular shift. Every night is a different cab. There are no assigned cabs, except for senior drivers who've been there decades.

Next up: You walk out to the lot. Locate the cab. Inspect it. Check the fluids. Check the brake lights, headlights, windshield wipers. Make sure everything is working and clean. If something isn't right with the cab, you walk back inside and tell the shift leader what is wrong, so that you don't get blamed for it at the end of your shift. When you're done inspecting the cab, you notify the dispatcher over the CB radio that you are ready to roll out and begin the shift.

From there, you spend the next twelve hours fielding calls. All night. No breaks unless you have to piss in an alley or eat a gas station hot dog on the go. Around 4 a.m., sometimes later, the dispatcher notifies you that your shift is over and to bring your cab back to the cabstand for shift change.

Before the end of the shift, each driver is required to refuel, wash, and vacuum their assigned cab.

This is my job.

I am now a cabdriver.

TRAINING DAY

Before being turned loose with a cab, newly hired drivers must spend their first shift riding along with a veteran driver. The seasoned driver instructs the new driver in the do's and don'ts of the job and answers any questions the new driver may have. My trainer's name is Billy. He has a carefully groomed mustache similar to that of a middle-aged cop. It makes him appear older than his thirty-two years.

"I've got a baby face. That's not good," he says. "People think they can get one over on you."

We field calls throughout the night.

Billy chain smokes. And talks a lot.

"I've been driving for five years straight."

We begin picking up and dropping off passengers. He seems very familiar with many of the passengers.

"They're regulars."

Billy lights another cigarette and stomps on the accelerator.

"I got dirt on everybody in this town. Drugs, sex, gambling, strip clubs. Whatever. Everybody's got dirt."

He likes to talk about women.

"I like sex. You can get laid in the cab. Not a lot, but you'll get some."

At random intervals, Billy groans and reaches under the seat. He surfaces with a can of Lysol and sprays it aimlessly around the cab.

"Most cabs smell like shit. You've got to keep them fresh. You make better tips with a clean cab."

Like many of the drivers I'll meet in the coming year, he is a chain-smoker.

"I smoke all night. Keeps you alert."

He makes no connection between smoking and a smelly cab.

"I just roll down the window."

According to Billy's research, 70 percent of the cab business is local people who don't have a car and can't afford to buy one.

"Poor people just trying to get to work."

The city bus system is inadequate.

"It stops running at 10 p.m. So people take cabs."

Another 20 percent of the passengers are travelers coming and going from the airport or Greyhound bus station.

"The last 10 percent is people with DUIs or those looking to avoid DUIs."

One trip—a pick-up and drop-off—with a passenger is referred to as a "call."

"You'll get good calls, bad calls, and everything in between. Don't sweat the bad calls. But watch out if you get too many good calls."

Why?

"The other drivers will start to hate you. They're crazy jealous, especially if you're a new driver getting good calls. They'll think you got something going on with the dispatcher."

Like what?

"They'll think you're fucking her or him."

Billy logs all his calls in a notebook. Each entry includes the call's address, drop-off location, and the total cost of each fare. There are no meters in Lafayette cabs. The cost of each fare is determined by the dispatcher who references a proprietary formula that incorporates the distance traveled in and out of the city and state limits.

Why don't the cabs have meters?

"I think people complained too much about them. That's my guess. They'd stare at the price of the fare going up while they were stopped at a light, and they'd go crazy, complaining. Plus, Lafayette traffic is so bad at peak hours that I think it just made things worse, so now the dispatchers just estimate everything by distance traveled on a gridded map of the city."

While stopped at a traffic light, Billy rips a sheet of paper from his notebook and feverishly writes on it. He tosses it in my lap.

"These are your call signs."

What are they for?

"That's how you communicate with the dispatcher. Those are the CB radio codes like what cops use. It's like shorthand."

CB Radio Codes:
10-1 = I am exiting the cab.
10-2 = I am back in the cab.
10-3 = Repeat the transmission.
10-4 = Yes/Affirmative.
10-5 = My cab is empty and available.
10-6 = Call the police. Emergency code for dispatcher to the police.

While lighting another cigarette, Billy holds down the horn, merges into traffic, and screams at a motorist.

"Fuck off!" He exhales. "People are assholes."

He points in the rearview mirror and gesticulates, riled up in some silent exchange with the offending motorist.

"Don't 10-6 unless you have a real emergency."

How often do driver's use the 10-6 code?

"Happens all the time," he says. "People run on you. Try to rob you. Sometimes a fare will refuse to pay. All kinds of shit."

Why would they not want to pay?

"They're drunk or crazy and think you are overcharging them."

How often does that happen?

"A lot. People complain about everything. You'll see. People are nuts."

During the first four hours of the shift, Billy picks up and drops off a couple dozen customers and meticulously logs each trip in his notebook that he keeps at his side.

"If you're not dicking around, you'll run forty calls in a night."

What qualifies as dicking around?

"Farting off. Not answering the radio. Smoking crack. Going to your house, taking a nap."

Do drivers do that kind of stuff?

"Oh, yeah. All the time. Drivers are crazy. But night shift drivers are the craziest of the bunch. Who else wants to drive around all night in the ghettos with strangers and nutjobs trying to rob you?"

What about smoking crack?

"There are a couple night drivers that do stuff. They just haven't been caught yet. You'll see who's who. Oh, and most everybody's on pills. Not all, but most."

What kind of pills?

"Painkillers. Why? You got any?"

Billy winks and steers the cab into a parking lot, swerving around pedestrians.

"I'm joking, but if you come across some let me know."

He stops at the front entrance to a grocery store. He flicks his cigarette out the window. We wait.

What else do I need to know?

"The dispatchers are going to hate you. Mostly because you are new and don't know what you're doing. They're all assholes. But you have to tolerate them."

Why?

"They're the ones that make you money. They decide who gets what calls. They'll fuck you over hard if you get on their bad side. They'll have you running five-dollar calls all night. And if they think you're fucking off on the job, they'll send you home."

Do they do this with all new drivers?

"Oh, yeah. They treat you like shit, but that's part of the deal."

Yeah?

"They're hard on new drivers. They'll try to make you quit; send you on a gang of shit calls. Just to see if you're built for this kind of job. Insult you over the radio. Make you feel stupid."

That bad?

"Half the new drivers quit in the first week. You just have to bite your tongue. Stay cool. Say 10-4 a lot."

How long does this rite of passage last?

"About two weeks and then, if you're still around, they lay off and treat you normal."

I nod.

"You'll get the hang of it."

We roll through the remainder of Billy's shift, picking up and dropping off dozens of passengers. Repeat. Again. And again. Over and over. Billy's multitasking skills are impressive. He flies up and down the streets, dodging pedestrians while fetching loose change from his rumpled pockets, making conversation with passengers, and randomly jerking the steering wheel to maintain control. He does this all while occasionally talking to the dispatcher and writing down addresses and fares on his meticulously organized call sheet.

It's simultaneously frightening, bizarre, and fairly remarkable.

"I ain't dicking around. I'm here to work and make money."

It looks like you're doing pretty good at it.

"I am. I'm one of the top-earning drivers. They know I get shit done."

We plow through the rest of the evening, picking up and dropping approximately forty to fifty passengers. There's very little downtime. If any. We don't even stop to eat.

"I eat on the run. Grab some food at a drive-thru and keep rolling."

What if you get tired?

"I smoke a cigarette. Or eat a pill."

Is that a normal kind of thing on the night shift?

"Like I said, everybody on the night shift is crazy. That's why they work nights."

Yeah?

"Absolutely. And the ones who aren't crazy, they work the day shift."

Around 4 a.m., at the end of the shift, Billy fills the cab with gas and then drives to a self-serve car wash. He jumps out and wildly sprays down the whole cab. Suds. Water flying. He also vacuums the interior, pulling out loose change, pocket combs, toothpicks, and other crap that's become wedged in the back seat over the course of the night's fares. It's all done in less than five minutes. With that mandatory task completed, we speed back to the cab-stand to turn in the car, do paperwork, get cashed out.

"You get paid out every night. In cash. That's the best thing about the job. If you've got a light bill to pay, boom. Jump in the cab for the night and make that money."

I follow Billy into the cabstand. He goes into a side room where a night clerk checks his call sheet and paperwork. Billy hands him his gas receipt and the full amount of cash he's collected for the night's shift, minus tips. The night clerk calculates the total of Billy's fares and then hands him back $150. The shift is officially over.

"That's it. We're done."

Billy heads for the parking lot. I thank him for the job-related wisdom and say goodnight.

"You got any other questions?"

None that I can think of.

"Good. The rest you have to learn on your own."

FIRST NIGHT ON THE JOB

I arrive at the cabstand an hour early for my first shift. After completing some final, driver-related paperwork, I am assigned a "permanent driver number."

"You will be Driver #4," says Joe, my boss.

"Never use your real name on the radio. Just your number."

Why?

"You don't want people to *know* who you are," he says cryptically.

Confused, I nod.

Why number four?

"It's available."

I nod again.

It's my first night alone in the cab. It is Friday and the first of the month.

"Weekends are very busy," says Joe. "And customers get paid on the first, so it is extra busy."

I write my name on the night shift driver roster and wait around the day room. Drivers mull around, smoking cigarettes, making small talk. Day drivers return from their shifts. They walk in and hand their keys to the shift leader who promptly passes them to the next night driver in line who promptly walks out the door to begin his or her shift.

Eventually, I am assigned a cab. I walk out into the afternoon daylight and locate my cab for the evening. I inspect it, checking the lights, oil, interior, exterior, and all the other things mentioned during my driver orientation. After strapping in and starting the cab, I key the mic on the CB radio and alert the dispatcher that I am "10-5" (empty and available for calls).

"10-4, Number Four."

The dispatcher sends me on a series of short calls. Within the first two hours, I quickly learn it is a madhouse out there. Customers getting fucked up. Drugged up. Cracked up. Drunk. And whatever else they can think of. It's humanity in its strangest and most ridiculous modern incarnation. Just as Billy, my trainer, had predicted, the dispatchers give me a hard time.

"What's taking you so damn long, Number Four?!"

"You're dragging! Hurry it up!"

"Speak up! I can't hear you, Number Four. You got a problem talking into the radio?!"

It is a humbling experience.

On my fourth call of the night, a man loads a giant TV into the backseat of the cab and asks that I take him to a motel.

OK.

The TV is huge. It takes up two-thirds of the back seat.

"I'm going to sell this TV. I'll pay you with the money."

I raise an eyebrow and roll with it. When we arrive at the motel, the man's contact does not want to buy the TV, which means the guy does not have the money to pay me for the fare.

This is my real first lesson on the job: if a customer cannot pay the fare, the driver must pay it. That's the rule at the cabstand. The driver eats any loses, aside from being robbed. No exceptions.

I shake my head and leave the guy in a parking lot. But I keep the TV as collateral and drive off with it, TV wobbling around like a whale in the back seat of the cab.

The dispatcher gives me a call to pick up in a residential neighborhood.

I roll.

When I arrive, three women attempt to get in the cab. They see the massive TV in the backseat.

"Oh, no, honey. We can't fit in there."

I exit the cab, remove the TV from the back seat, and leave it on the curb. Merry Christmas to someone out there. I roll on, fielding calls and bouncing around the city, slowly getting the feel of the job. I'm sent into neighborhoods and down strange backstreets that I've never even heard of. You can never know all of a city. There's always more to the mystery. It's everywhere. Around every corner. You pass it every day. But you don't notice it until you have to stop and look at it.

I finish the shift around 4:30 a.m. I fuel up, wash, and vacuum the cab. After cashing out and doing paperwork with the night clerk, I take home $89 for shift.

I drive back to my motel room.

I take a shower and slowly fall asleep, content that I am, once again, a productive member of society.

THE JOURNEY

I'm two weeks into the job and adjusting to the vampire-like pull of the night shift. Five nights a week. I work all night and then sleep most of the day. I wake around 2 p.m. and then return to the cabstand and do it again. Aside from the inevitable learning curve and the blistering reprimands of the dispatchers, it's not too bad for a shit job.

I like the randomness of it.

I like the weirdos and strangers.

I like prowling through all corners of the night.

I like being left alone to do the job.

I like not having a boss over my shoulder.

I like the action.

I like the ghettos.

I like the people.

I like hearing their stories.

This job is just what I need at this point in my life.

I have nothing else.

I'm a musician with no band.

So fuck it.

I'm on a new adventure.

And whatever I do,

 Whatever the adventure is,

  I always make it into art.

  This is the only way

  I can deal with the humbling nature of my life.

Thus, I'm going to make this job my new art project: Cabdriver.

Each day is a masterpiece and I'm going to paint every detail of it.

I will dive into the bowels of the slaughterhouse

And roll around in the muck

That cakes the floors there.

I will push myself to explore

New people and experiences.

The crippling narcissism

That plagues many artists

Such as myself

Will be replaced
With a thorough exploration of them,
The passengers.
I will look at every truth,
    no matter how dark
        and accept it for what it is.

I will learn about these people of the night shift
and I will learn from them
    and in turn
    I will learn about myself
        even when it is painful.
    I want to know.
I want to smash my face
Right up against
The ass of this world
And see what is there.

NO CRACK IN CAB

Pick up: Greyhound bus station. The passenger is a boat worker of Asian descent. A fisherman. He asks to sit up front. I wave him in. He's going to Intracoastal City, Louisiana. It's a sixty-five-dollar fare. We roll. On the drive, we make small talk. He wrestles with the language, speaking in broken English and stunted phrases. As we're exiting city limits, he leans in close and whispers to me.

"Can you get me the crack?"

Get you the what?

"The crack."

Crack? As in crack cocaine?

"Yes, I want the crack."

I shake my head and politely tell him no, I cannot get him "the crack."

"You no like the crack?" he asks.

No, I don't. I no like the crack.

He pauses.

Stares out the window a few minutes.

Then he returns to the subject.

"You no understand. I get crack for me!"

Oh, no. I do understand exactly what you want. But I don't have it, nor do I know where to get it.

"Yes! Me know where to get much crack. I smoke crack then I go boat. You see. We go?"

I sigh.

No, you not see, buddy.

No crack in cab, I emphasize.

I cannot let you bring the crack in the cab.

He stares at me in disbelief.

"One crack! Then we go."

I repeat, louder. NO CRACK IN CAB!

Although I've experimented with many drugs in the past, I've never done or been interested in crack. During these first few weeks of driving a cab, I've witnessed an overwhelming amount of people on drugs. Many of them, addicted to crack. It's heartbreaking and tragic. The demographic of users is massive.

15

Young. Old. Rich. Poor.
White. Black. Hispanic. Asian.
Yuppies. Vagabonds. Executives. Thugs. Rednecks. Housewives.
Very sad.
And a very rough life.
We roll on.

"Can you stop in Abbeville?" he asks. "I need to stop at my friend house."
Are you going to buy crack?
"No! No crack! Just talk. To my friend."
OK.
"It's my brother house. I need to talk with him."
The stop is on the way.
I'm fairly certain the guy is going to buy crack, but I can't prove it, so we go where he wants to go. I locate the apartment complex where he wants to stop. I park outside his "brother's" apartment. Asian guy goes in.
Five minutes later, he comes out and climbs back in the cab.
But this time, instead of sitting up front with me, he sits in the back seat.
"I sit in back to relax now."
I nod.
We roll.
As we get out of the city and down the marshes along Intracoastal Highway, I see a flicker of light in the back seat. I turn around. Asian guy is holding a pipe to his lips and smoking what I assume is his newly acquired crack in the back seat.
NO CRACK IN CAB! I yell.
"Yeah, yeah, I know, I know," he says. "You no like the crack,"
I know I don't like the crack, but you cannot do that in the cab!
I pull the cab to the side of the road.
Get out! I tell him.
"OK, I won't do the crack."
No crack in the cab!
"What if I blow smoke out window?"
He points to the window.
No crack in the cab!
You done?
"Yeah, let's go. No crack in cab."
Correct!
We roll in silence.

The darkness of the Louisiana marsh surrounds us.

Wind whistling through the windows.

We arrive at his destination: a dilapidated trailer, parked among old fishing boats floating in the brackish water of the Gulf of Mexico.

"I call you next time I need cab."

OK, buddy. Just remember my number one rule.

"No crack in cab!"

Correct!

And with that, the Asian man walks off into the opaque Louisiana night to enjoy the simple pleasures of deep-sea fishing and the smoking of crack.

CHICKEN BONES

I drop off four people
At an apartment complex
In a north side ghetto.
As I'm attempting to exit the parking lot,
Some local, summertime thugs
Who are hanging out in said parking lot
Lazily block my exit.
Like regal lords of the wasteland.
They just stand there, in my way.
They've got nothing else to do
But hang around in a parking lot
And stare at the mongoloid sun.
One of them is shirtless
And eating fried chicken
From a fast food box.
I politely pump the horn a couple times
To signal that I desire passage
Through this sacred realm.
They mumble bitterly
And toss me snide glances.
The shirtless chicken thug
Seems very insulted.
He approaches the cab
And, in one fluid motion,
Lazily tosses his box
Of spent chicken bones
Across my windshield.
They slide down the glass.
Well, that's nice! I say.
We lock eyes,
Blankly staring at one another.
I click on the windshield wipers,
And drive around him
As chicken bones spill off
The front of the cab.

THE BLACK BAG

I pick up a guy at residence in a neighborhood called Fightville. He's carrying a black duffle bag. He gives me the address. It's a house on the north side of town. We roll in silence. He's not a very talkative passenger. All my attempts at small talk are met with a simple shrug of his shoulders.

As we near his destination, the passenger asks me to park down the street from the house and wait for him to return.

"I'll be right back."

He exits with the bag. He walks down the street and then strolls up the driveway of his destination. He places the black bag on the hood of a car parked in the garage of the house.

He turns and walks back to the cab.

He climbs in the front seat.

Are we done? I ask.

"Wait."

I put the cab back in PARK.

We sit in silence.

Both of us staring at the bag and then back at the house.

And then back at the bag.

And then the house.

Waiting.

What are we doing? I ask. Are we waiting for someone?

He dismisses my query with a condescending wave of his hand.

"Just chill."

Sigh.

Nothing happens.

We just stare into space.

Both of us glancing back and forth at the bag and the house.

No one comes out of the house. Nothing happens that I can notice.

He shifts in his seat.

"OK. We good. We can go."

Yeah? OK, great.

I don't ask questions in this case, because I don't think I would get any answers. At all.

I drop him off at the same place I picked him up.

He pays the fare and offers no explanation or tip.

HACK FACTS

The average lifespan of a taxicab is ten months. Most of them are old police cars bought at public auctions.

The average yellow light lasts about five seconds.

The first four-way traffic light was created in Detroit in 1920.

On an average night, a Lafayette cabdriver makes approximately $100 in take-home pay.

The average number of miles driven during a twelve-hour shift is 180–250 miles.

Driving a cab is the tenth most dangerous job in America.

In 1979, taxicab drivers won the right to charge an extra $0.50 for late-night fares.

In 1899, taxi driver Jacob German was the first person to be arrested for speeding in New York.

The average Lafayette fare is approximately six dollars.

The taxicab gets its name from the 1891 invention of the Taximeter, an instrument used to measure the distance and time a car travels.

Louisiana requirements for taxi operators include: Class D license and a chauffeur's permit issued by the city. Drivers must have no sex offenses and must be at least twenty-one years of age. They must also have a clean driving record with no recent traffic violations, no major criminal convictions, and no DUI convictions.

THE DRUNKEN COWBOY

Call to pick up at a house. The passenger is drunk. Wasted. Male. Midfifties. Tall and skinny with a big cowboy hat.

Where are you going, buddy?

"I'm going to fuck me a twenty-two-year-old."

OK, what's the address?

"It's up the road. I'll show you."

We roll.

"I was a sniper in Vietnam."

How many people did you kill?

"Twelve or fourteen. I don't want to talk about it," he says. "If I talk about it, they'll kill me."

Who are they?

"Don't you worry about it."

Who is the woman you are going to meet?

"Some hot little thing I met at Mardi Gras."

Nice girl?

"She knows how to ride a dick."

She knows you're coming over tonight, right?

"No, I'm going to surprise her."

I raise an eyebrow. This might not go well. He ignores the comment. We roll on. He talks. His favorite topics are women, drinking, and sex. When he sees me taking notes on our conversation in the margins of my call sheet, he asks what I'm writing. A suicide note, I tell him. He nods and puffs his cigarette. Blows it out in a weary haze.

"Been there."

We arrive at his destination. It's a small trailer in a crowded Breaux Bridge trailer park. There is a truck and a small car parked outside the trailer. Cowboy exits the cab and knocks on the door. I wait in the cab and watch, sitting low in the seat. A guy opens the door. He's a big guy. They converse. I can't hear what they're saying but the body language indicates it is not friendly banter.

Big Guy gestures and yells, "Get the fuck out of here!"

Cowboy stiffens up, offended.

They cuss at one another a bit.

Big Guy steps out, grabs Cowboy, and gives him a forceful shove. Cowboy trips and falls to the ground in a drunken heap, sliding in the dewy grass. Big Guy stands there, waiting to see what Cowboy will do. Cowboy slowly rises, brushes himself off, and walks away.

Good move.

Cowboy stumbles back to the cab. Dejected. Big Guy surveys his exit and stares angrily at both of us. I put the cab in DRIVE. Cowboy and I roll back to town in silence. It's an odd silence, punctuated only by the droning hum of the road. Cowboy slumps in his seat, smokes, and gazes into the night. We pass a farm and some cattle.

You can always go fuck a cow, I tell him.

Cowboy looks at me.

"Yeah, I could, but then I'd have to walk around to kiss her."

THE SCORNED WOMAN

2:11 a.m. Closing time. Cruising downtown. I see a woman standing in the street outside of a nightclub. Midforties. She flags me down and climbs in the back seat.

Where to?

"I'm going to Abbeville."

Forty-minute drive.

We roll.

She is quiet. Near silent. Under the crackle of the CB radio, I hear her crying. Brokenhearted sobbing. Nothing is sadder than a crying woman.

What's wrong? I ask.

"I don't want to talk about it."

A few minutes later, she really begins to bawl. Loudly.

"I'm only going to tell you this once," I say. "Something is troubling you. You're going to talk. And I'm going to listen. We've got a long drive. So, you may as well talk to me."

She proceeds to tell me how she's been married fifteen years. They have one child. She's been faithful to her husband throughout the marriage. She recently discovered that he has been having an affair for the past five years. Maybe longer. Maybe the whole time. She and her husband came out tonight. Together. Dinner, drinks. Months ago, she hired a private investigator who gathered "undeniable evidence" that her husband was cheating on her. Tonight, after she'd had a few drinks, she gathered the courage to confront him about the infidelity.

She asked him about the woman. Her husband became upset. They argued. He confirmed some of the accusations. He admitted he had been cheating on her and that he wanted a divorce.

Then he stood up and left her at the bar.

Alone.

Crying.

And broken.

"I'm devastated."

She doesn't think she is pretty anymore.

"No one will want me now," she says. "I'm too old."

More sobbing.

"I'm too old to be alone."

So, she ignored his betrayals as her self-esteem crumbled into the dirt and she began drinking to combat the agony of each day. She watched him slip farther away into his own lies. And he, in turn, began using her drinking as leverage to crush her further into the dirt and excuse his own vices even though he was an alcoholic himself. That's how it works sometimes; we twist the knives into each other's weaknesses while cloaking our own so as to steady our own distorted sense of reality.

We point out each other's faults, because we know them as our own.

And we demonize them accordingly.

Another year arrives.

Here comes another anniversary.

But she remains faithful to him and the lie.

"Everyone in my office is fucking someone else."

She thinks about joining them.

"But that's not me. I don't want that."

So, she doesn't mention anything until tonight when she confronts him. And he tells her that he is leaving her for good and that he is taking their kid. Period.

He leaves her there.

Alone.

At the bar.

Walks out.

Forever.

And she finds herself surrounded by people who are laughing.

Not at her.

They're just loud. Yelling.

Drinking.

Celebrating something.

Something she doesn't care about.

She exits the bar. Crying. Inconsolable.

She calls a cab.

I pick her up.

This is where I find her sobbing in the back seat.

We arrive at her house. I pull into the driveway. Turn off the ignition. Park. She continues to talk. Giving me more details. The hidden notes. The gut feelings. The investigator, checking license plates. The credit card bill with hotel charges.

The emotional distance.

The time he picked her up at the airport and was drunk and not even happy to see her.

She ignored it. But didn't forget it.

I sit and listen to her talk.

Sometimes that is the only thing you can do for people:

Just give them your silence

And listen.

THE ONE-ARMED MAN

1:54 a.m. The bars are closing. I get a call to pick up at DJ's Bar. It's a hole-in-the-wall in an industrial park. I roll up. Honk. Nobody comes out. I turn off the cab. Walk in. Place is nearly empty except for the bartender and a few patrons, one of whom is a one-armed man, perched on a barstool.

I ask the bartender who called the cab.

The bartender points at the one-armed man who idly raises his one arm and waves in my direction. He looks like an FM radio DJ from 1985. He's in his late forties. I approach and inform him that I am his cabdriver.

The One-Armed Man mumbles something unintelligible toward me.

Excuse me? I ask.

"What? You want a prize? You're a cabdriver. BIG FUCKING DEAL!"

OK. I smile.

I'm parked outside, I say.

I walk toward the exit.

He drunkenly follows.

I open the rear door to the cab.

"Ah, no," he says. Shakes his head and mulishly shoves the door closed. "I always ride up front."

He walks around and climbs in the front passenger seat.

Where to?

"I'll show you."

He fires up a cigarette and takes a long, self-absorbed drag. He stares out the window and appears very annoyed.

"Where are you from?" he asks, sneeringly.

I'm from here, I reply.

"Where is here?"

Here as in Lafayette, I say.

"No, I mean, like, where are you *from*?"

Look, dude, I'm from here.

I live here.

I work here.

I pay taxes here.

And I have a rule: I only answer the same question twice. After that, you're on your own.

"Oh! Is that how it is?!"

Oh, man. The One-Armed Man doesn't like that answer at all. He spits cigarette smoke and drunkenly slurs, "What kind of shit *is* that?"

I'm not sure what you are asking me.

He goes silent for a few minutes.

"What kind of music do you listen to?"

Music? All kinds of music. I like metal.

"Metal?! You ever heard of Gangster?" he asks.

Sort of. Apparently, Gangster was a Lafayette hair metal band from the 1980s.

"Sort of, huh? Well, they were great."

Silence.

"They kicked ass!" he exclaims. "Not like this pussy shit you people listen to now."

Silence.

The One-Armed Man grows increasingly annoyed. He blows more smoke out of the window. In a bossy tone, he directs me to his home's address.

"Slow down! You missed the turn!"

"Left. I said take a LEFT!"

"Now go straight ahead two blocks."

"You're going too fast."

After ten minutes of patiently tolerating his bullshit, he's starting to annoy the shit out of me.

I pull the cab over and stop.

OK, buddy, I say. Don't tell me how to drive and I won't tell you how to blow dry your hair.

He looks at me strangely.

"What kind of shit is *that*?!"

We pull up to his house.

"Thank God it's over."

I tell him the fare is seven dollars.

"Wait here. I don't have any cash on me."

I'm guessing he drank it all. He exits the cab and walk in his house. I wait. Ten minutes later, he returns. He motions for me to roll down the window.

I roll it down.

And like some feudal overlord, throwing rotten turnips to a peasant, the One-Armed Man tosses the money in the window. It scatters across the seat. He loftily turns on his heel and walks off, strutting away as if to say, "Fuck off, loser. I may have lost my arm, but NEVER MY PRIDE."

What a strange, but entertainingly odd guy.

I laugh to myself and continue with the shift.

It's late. Things are winding down. I'm nearing the end of my shift when I get a call from the dispatcher.

"Hey, Driver Four. I just got a complaint from a customer."

I laugh to myself.

Yeah, what is it?

"That guy you dropped off in the Saint streets. He's a regular. He says you were rude and drove badly."

I shake my head.

Rude?

What kind of shit is *that?*

ROADKILL WILLIE

Call to pick up at a redneck bar. Two guys come out. Forty to fifty years old. Drunk, hard-grizzled rednecks. They look like scarecrow buzzards. Leather-skinned. Missing teeth. They pile in the back seat.

What are y'all doing tonight? I ask.

"We're in town working construction."

Where to?

"Desperado's Strip Club."

We roll. They make small talk in the back.

"My name's Trent and guess what? My buddy here is Britney Spears's uncle!"

Yeah?

I look over at the guy. He's a short fellow. Tan and wiry.

"I'm from Kentwood," he says, proudly. "The press call me Roadkill Willie."

Is that right?

"I'm the brother of Britney's father."

Willie talks as we roll.

"Justin Timberlake's a pussy, but, man, that motherfucker can sing."

We roll on.

"My brother almost kicked her baby daddy's ass! He's a bum."

I drop them off at their destination: the strip club.

I continue fielding the night's calls. Roughly three hours later, the dispatcher calls me on the radio.

"Remember them two guys you dropped off at Desperados?"

Yep.

"Well, they just called and want you to go pick them up again."

10-4.

I whip the cab around and head north on I-49.

When I arrive at the strip club, neither of them is outside.

That means I have to park the cab, go in, find them, and then extract them. It's always a little harder when guys like that are extremely drunk. It's like babysitting monsters.

I park and enter the club.

Typical strip club scene.

Music blasting.

Strippers dancing.

A lot of dudes are walking around.

I navigate through the crowd, looking for the Roadkill Boys. Out of the corner of my eye, I see someone drunkenly scissor-stepping toward the men's room. Good news: it's Trent, Roadkill Willie's partner. I grab him.

Where's Willie? I ask.

He points at the stage.

I look over and see Willie, feeding money to a stripper onstage.

I grab Trent by the shirt and navigate over to Willie.

I tap Willie on the shoulder and yell in his ear.

Hey, man! Time to go!

"Let's do it!" yells Willie.

They are both trashed.

I grab each of them by the arm and lead them out of the club. We pile in the cab and roll. Destination: a bombed-out trailer park on the other side of town. I'm familiar with it from dropping off customers at this same destination, which is kind of like a mining camp for hardcore longshot, manual-labor types. It's a twenty-minute drive.

They make small talk and fade in and out of consciousness.

Drunk and trashed. Nothing interesting of note is produced in the conversation.

When we arrive, they pay me. They even tip me a few dollars. They pile out and I watch them stumble off and disappear into the dark.

As a last thought, I ask what they are going to do for the rest of the night.

Willie turns to me.

"Probably smoke a rock."

BROKEBACK

I pick up two dudes at a shit-kicker bar. They're from Oklahoma. And they're drunk and obnoxious. They play baseball for the local university. University of Louisiana. They both make mention of my long hair.

"You a hippie?"

Nope.

"You ain't one of those peace freaks, huh?"

Maybe.

One guy goes on a long, drunken rant about the other guy being "his boy."

"Charlie's my boy. He's got my back."

That's great.

"I got his. And he got mine," he says. "Anybody messes with him, they got to fuck with me!"

These guys are almost intolerable.

Their chummy, brochacho camaraderie of aggressive masculinity reeks of homophobia and an adolescence filled with doling out geek beatdowns. These are the kind of dudes you want to open-hand slap really hard—just once—in some equally aggressive attempt to get them to wake up from whatever belligerent reality they've been living for the last twenty years.

In the most demented, redneck drawl I can muster, I turn around and look at them.

Y'all ain't a couple queers, huh?! I say.

They didn't like that.

At all.

THE OLD-TIMERS

Cabdrivers are some weird characters. Truly an unusual breed. There are a couple war vets. An ex-draft dodger. One acid casualty. Some masturbatory eccentrics. There's even a cross-dressing driver named Earl who wears a down vest all summer long with rubber tits and bra on underneath it. No bullshit. He's also missing two front teeth, is bald on top, and has long stringy hair. He's kind of scary when you bump into him during shift-change in the pre-dawn hours. There's a gang of degenerate gamblers that hit the video poker casinos during lulls in the shift.

And there are indeed a couple of crack-addicted drug dealers, one of whom is a forty-something-year-old black guy that is built like a massive football player. He's wild. His name is Houston and he's a top earner, sometimes pulling in $500 per shift. Unbelievable. I think that's why he's tolerated. When he is not making crazy money running other crack addicts and prostitutes around the city in his cab, he occasionally goes AWOL during his shift, takes the cab and disappears. The rumor is that he hides out in motels with prostitutes and smokes crack all night, so fried that he is unable to return to his shift and too freaked out to bring the cab back in for fear he'll be arrested.

The other driver who is suspected of dealing and smoking drugs in the cab is a sixty-four-year-old man named Lonnie from Abbeville. This guy is already a legend in the cab just for his crazy antics, which include pulling in big money nights like Houston where he makes $500-600 per shift. He often blows this money shortly thereafter and much like Houston, disappears for days with the cab while allegedly smoking crack with hookers in motels. He always shows back up at the cabstand, apologetically pleading his case. Both of these guys have been fired and rehired numerous times, because of their massive earnings for the business.

There's another weird driver named Captain Mustache. He's got a massive mustache and is rumored to be a Peeping Tom.

There's Russel who is an ex-carney and all-around weird guy. I went to his house one time to give him a ride to work and his whole apartment was covered in dirty clothes. Underwear and soiled T-shirts everywhere.

There are a few ex-truck drivers, ex-teachers, ex-salesmen, ex-weed farmers. From what I can gather, the majority of them have some deep-seated problems—usually an anger or anti-authority issue—that has pushed them to the fringes of society and thus the gloomy darkness of the night shift.

I think my favorite drivers are the old-timers. Some of these guys have been working the roads for forty years or longer. There are legendary stories of these individuals—past and present—that circulate among the drivers. For example, there was a driver in the 1970s named Bonaventure. His skill level at "cutting calls" is mythic. "Cutting a call" is when you pick someone up off the street, drive them to their destination, charge them a fare, but never call it into the cab company, thus the company makes no money on the fare even though you are on the clock and their taxi. This is an offense so great that if you are caught, you are immediately fired. Bonaventure once allegedly cut a call all the way to Houston, Texas. He claimed his wife was sick in the hospital and notified the dispatcher that he was going to check on her. He didn't call the dispatcher back for seven hours, not because his wife was sick, but because he cut that call to Houston and kept the money.

My favorite old-timer is Dale. He's six-foot-two and bone skinny. The nicest guy ever, but he takes no bullshit. His brother Bud is one of the dispatchers. They've both been in the cab business for decades. They've seen it all in the cabs.

"I've been driving since the roads were made of dirt."

Like many cabdrivers, they're also both pill-poppers.

"I take what I need."

On the subject of passengers, Dale is very opinionated:

"Don't let assholes in your cab."

If he doesn't like someone, he kicks them out of the cab. If they are rude, he doesn't even let them get in. He drives away.

"Always trust your gut. No matter what the situation. If it feels wrong, it is wrong."

What do you do if it feels wrong?

"Leave them standing at the curb. I drive off and turn up the radio."

What if it's a woman?

"Well, if she's crazy and she's already in your cab acting crazy and she won't leave, you have to grab her by the hair and drag her out."

What?

"It's the only thing that works."

You sure?

"Trust me. You can't reason with a crazy woman. They're very dangerous."

I don't know if I could do something like that.

"Oh, trust me. You do this job long enough, you will. You're going to do a lot of things you never thought you'd ever do. You won't be proud of it, but you'll do it. Guaranteed. It's just part of the job, unfortunately."

I nod and stare into the distance.

"Trust me, if you don't do what I tell you, you could end up dead."

FIRE & RAIN

I've seen fire and I've seen rain, but I've never had the pleasure of seeing James Taylor live. He's playing in town tomorrow night at the Cajundome, Lafayette's arena. Early in the shift, the dispatcher gives me a call to pick up at a local restaurant.

Who is there when I arrive? The guys in James Taylor's band.

They cram inside the cab. James Taylor is not with them. But one of the guys in the band is Blue Lou Marini. He's the long-haired saxophone player who was in the *Blues Brothers* movie, the Saturday Night Live Band, and Blood, Sweat & Tears. I make small talk with them and mention I'm a musician as well. The keyboard player expresses an interest in Cajun and zydeco music as well as some accordion lessons, so I call my old buddy Steve Riley. He's an extremely talented, Grammy-winning, Cajun accordionist and songwriter who lives in the area. I arrange for the two of them to meet up and hang out.

When I drop off the James Taylor guys at their hotel, the keyboard guy shows his appreciation by giving me two backstage passes to the show tomorrow. I show my appreciation by thanking him and selling the tickets later that night for fifty dollars to a friend's parents.

I'm not a big James Taylor fan, but his band are nice guys.

LUMP IN MY THROAT

Pick-up: grocery store. The passenger: a nice old lady that lives right in the middle of a crime-infested ghetto. As we turn onto her block, the street is full of loitering thug-types and street-level drug dealers. Many of them are standing in the street in front of her house. I steer the cab around them.

They sneer at us. She sighs as we pull in the driveway.

"Those children."

I pop the trunk and unload her groceries, carrying the bags into her house. She thanks me and pays the fare. She even tries to tip me with what money she has left: a dollar and change. She reaches out with her shaky, little hand to give it to me.

I feel a lump forming in my throat.

I refuse it. Keep it for another time, I say.

Such a sweet little lady, living in the patchwork streets of the ghetto against the stained glass of broken bottles and crime lights.

I say goodbye and walk back to the cab, keeping a vigilant eye on the drug dealers in front of her house. As I'm crossing her yard, I accidentally step in a hole in the grass and twist the shit out of my ankle. To keep from breaking it, I stop, drop, and roll in the grass.

When I come to a stop, I am staring at the sky.

Flat on my back.

I hear the guys in the street laughing. They think this is hilarious.

"Look that cabdriver done busted his ass!"

"Y'all see that dumb motherfucker trip?"

I bite my lip.

I wish I could say I told them all to FUCK OFF.

But I didn't.

Instead, I just stood up, brushed myself off,

And quietly walked back to the cab

With a different kind

Of lump

In my throat.

THE HIVE

Deep in the pre-dawn hours,
Under the eerie parade of stars
And above the catacomb sewers,
You can hear the city hum.
It is the hushed hum of a city asleep,
Radiating like a buzzing hive,
With the industrial drone
Of machines howling in the distance,
Rattling in the alleyways
As the Rorschach shadows
Uncoil their arms
And recede into the low tide
Of night.
This is the hidden underbelly
Of the city,
Where dope fiends
Gather at corner vigils,
Where third-strike alcoholics
Exhaust all the good graces
Of their families and friends,
Where whores, thieves, and
Drifters roam the wilds,
Melting into the brick, tar, and rotting wood
Of the hood.
I think
I was put here
On this earth
To listen
To the screaming serenade
Of these sirens,
Howling
Like homing beacons
For the forgotten.

THE ZYDECO PIRATE

Call to pick up at El Sido's Zydeco Club. Place is packed. I blow the horn. Out comes an older, stocky black man. Midsixties. Looking slightly inebriated. Dancing a little bit on his walk. I signal him with the horn. Over here, buddy. He climbs in and slurs out his address, but he is so drunk, I can't understand him.

He repeats the address: "418 Florence Avenue."

Got it.

But I can't recall off the top of my head where that street is located, so I pull out my map. This aggravates the old man.

"Put that away," he says. "I'll show you where it's at."

OK. I toss the map aside and we roll.

There's only one problem. I quickly realize from the arbitrary nature of his directions that this guy is too drunk to know where the hell he lives. Thus begins a strange ritual where he tells me where to go, I follow his lead and then we get lost. Repeat. I follow his lead. And then we get lost. Again. We repeat this ritual several more times. Finally, I lose my patience and pull the cab over to the curb.

I grab the map.

"You don't need that motherfucking map!"

Well, it seems like I do.

He begins cursing and berating me. While he's doing this, he punctuates his sentences with dramatic kicks to the floorboard of the cab. While he is having his fit, I ignore him and search the map for his address. This makes him angrier.

Finally, I locate his house on the map and aim the cab toward his address. With each turn, he curses louder and louder, totally convinced I'm going the wrong way.

That is until I pull into his driveway and we are looking at his house.

He stares blankly for a minute, silently registering the house in his brain.

"That's my house!"

Yes, it is!

I tell him the fare: five dollars.

"Oh, I don't owe you nothing!"

No, sir. I think you do.

"OK, you can tell the cops."

No problem. I make a show of pulling out my cell phone and dialing the police.

"How much did you say the fare was?"

"Five dollars."

He pays.

I roll.

I'm quickly learning that this is not unusual.

MOSS STREET PROJECTS

It's summertime. The heat is unbearable. Making people crazy. I get a call to pick up at the Moss Street Projects. I roll up to Building 6. I pump the horn a couple times, just to let them know I've arrived.

Out of nowhere, a crazy, shirtless, and profusely sweating man runs up to the cab and screams at me.

"Don't be honking your goddamn horn up in here like it's the Fourth of July! Motherfuckers get killed for that! You hear me motherfucker? You ain't the ice cream man! Get the fuck out of here!"

I give him my best poker face and quickly pull away, trying to avoid a serious confrontation.

I drive around the block to kill a few minutes. I circle back around to the pick-up address.

When I return, I honk again. This time I honk with a polite, peppy, but not obnoxious beep of the horn. And I keep watch for the crazy guy who ran up on me earlier.

Thankfully, he's nowhere in sight.

Maybe he had to go scare the shit out of someone else in the neighborhood.

IN THE RED

Tonight was one of those godforsaken shifts where the moon was full and everything that could possibly go wrong did exactly that. I plow through the first hour of the shift with the brutal summer sun pouring down all around me. Louisiana summers are unreal. Just brutal. After running a few dispatched calls, I notice that the thermostat on the cab is lurching into the RED. The cab is overheating. It's an older cab and running poorly.

I kick on the heater to pull some heat off the engine. An old trick, but in this case, it isn't working.

As I'm assessing the situation, the dispatcher calls.

"Driver Four, pick up the Tyler Mental Health Facility."

10-4.

I make the sign of the cross and roll to the destination. When I arrive, a guy in his early thirties exits the building and gets in the cab.

"I'm Timmy."

He's an odd bird. He talks incessantly.

We hit five-o'clock traffic and once again, the thermostat climbs into the RED. I hear the valves burbling under the hood. Coughing, sputtering. I shake my head and crank up the heater, again.

"Why's it so hot in here?"

I explain to Tim that the cab is overheating, and it may break down. So just sit tight. If it breaks down, I can call him another cab.

"This cab sucks!"

I don't disagree.

The dispatcher calls me over the radio, "Hurry it up, Driver Four! I've got more calls for you in that area."

I observe the heat gauge, climbing dangerously higher into the RED. It feels as if the radiator cap is about to launch to Mars. The cab sputters, jerks, and then finally it stalls in the middle of traffic. I try to restart it. Multiple times. It will not start. Traffic is backing up behind me. People are honking.

Meanwhile, Tim is in the back seat, babbling away the entire time.

"Do you believe in the occult?"

I roll my eyes. Not now, man.

The dispatcher calls again.

"Where you at, Number Four?"

I inform him the cab is dead in traffic.

"Dead? What happened?"

It overheated.

"Well, try to get it running. I'll check back on you."

Tim in the back seat is oblivious.

"My father was a seventh-degree pagan master. He's from the sacred order of Moloch. He told me that I would be one of the first telepaths to foretell the coming apocalypse."

Yep. I bet he was, buddy.

But I've got bigger problems than the apocalypse right now.

So please just shut the fuck up.

Bud, the dispatcher calls again.

"Did you say you were stalled in traffic?"

Affirmative.

Tim is still talking to me. "My grandmother was killed during the ancient witch hunts, but I inherited all her powers."

Dude just shut the fuck up, please!

Fun fact: crazy people are fairly useless in crisis situations.

I finally get the cab started and pull it into a gas station. I pop the hood and let the engine cool. This thing is about to blow. It whistles, burps, and spits foam from hoses. It's like a rabid beast. I wrap a rag around my fist and attempt to gradually ease off the radiator cap. But it's too hot. It's like defusing a bomb. And I'm not ready to die. Yet.

I locate a water hose behind the gas station and spray down the radiator. Engine included. It all spits, sizzles, and groans. I do this for fifteen minutes until the engine is finally cooled off, or at least not boiling hot. I refill the radiator with water.

"Are we going to make it to my house?" asks Tim.

Maybe. Say one of your prayers to Beelzebub, buddy. We're going to need it.

I crank up the cab.

It starts. Here we go. We roll like madmen to Tim's destination. He resumes babbling nonsensical nuttiness. Not again, bro. I try to ignore it. We weave and snake through traffic and by the grace of Satan's ass, we make it to Tim's house.

I drop him off. I'm overjoyed to be rid of him. If I'd had to listen to another ten minutes of him rambling on like that, I might have to start worshipping the Prince of Darkness, too.

Back to the journey.

I make a mad dash back toward the cabstand, approximately twelve miles away. It's an insane run. Shortly after takeoff, the thermostat gauge returns to the RED. And stays there for the entirety of the trip. The cab sputters and coughs, cursing satanic vexations at beasts unknown to this earthly realm.

I push the cab hard through traffic.

    Running yellow lights.

        Cutting through parking lots.

            Nearly hitting a couple of old ladies.

                Probably knocked a few years off their lives.

I fly down residential streets

    Like a demented race car.

        Foaming, frothing.

            Winning at nothing.

After dodging a few more red lights, I'm almost there. The cabstand comes into view. Thank God. I steer the heap into the yard and park it sloppily in a far corner of the lot as the radiator screams and steam pours from the engine. Good riddance.

I exit the cab and catch my breath.

Smoke a cigarette.

Nearby the sun is setting over a neighboring sewage pond.

It is almost beautiful.

No, it is beautiful.

The lather of clouds and the sun is reflecting off the gasoline and oil polluted water.

It's a rainbow in the wasteland.

I toss my cigarette and check in with the dispatcher.

"What the hell was going on out there?"

You don't want to know, Bud.

I don't think I could explain it anyway.

"That's life, pardner! Get back out there and ride."

I am assigned another cab. The new cab is not much better than the previous one. It is ragged and beat-up. There's a reason drivers show up early to work: to get the good cabs. The shit cabs are always the last to leave the lot.

I roll out and resume my shift. Two blocks away from the cabstand, I attempt to lower the driver's side window. Halfway down, the window jams. I bang on the side of the door to free it up, while cranking vigorously on the handle. The whole window apparatus makes a clunk sound, and then unceremoniously drops with a hollow thud into the bottom of the door.

No more window.

Went straight down.

It simply disappears off the hinge.

I stare into the distance. Expressionless. Unamused.

An hour later, en route to a call, I light a cigarette and glance in the side view mirror. At the same exact moment that I'm staring at my reflection and assessing my own ugliness on this day, the whole thing simply falls off the side of the cab and rolls down the street with a whimpering clang. I guess it came unglued or something.

I look back and see it rolling in the street.

I keep driving. There's no stopping now. I'm going all the way to the edge tonight, even if I have to kill every cab in the lot. I take a long and pensive drag on my cigarette and blow out the day's frustrations into the dead air of tomorrow.

I bang out the rest of the shift.

Sadly, and predictably in this case, the rest of the night does not get much better. In fact, at one point in this godforsaken shift, a crackhead passenger tries to pull out a chunk of my hair from the backseat after I refuse to stop at a gas station so she can buy beer. I have calls to pick up.

I have to put her out. Leave her at the curb.

Not long after that, a drunk man falls asleep in the back seat. I have to rouse him to get paid. Always a hassle.

"Where am I?" he asks.

You're in a cab. Outside your house. I'm your driver. The fare is fifteen dollars.

"Fifteen dollars? That's ridiculous."

Yep. It sure is.

It gets better. Near the end of the shift, a passenger's dog takes a crap in the back of the cab. The passenger doesn't even attempt to clean it up. Just leaves it sitting there. What an asshole.

It goes on and on like that. All night. I can't steer it away. I can't shake it off. The madness just keeps blooming and flowering in the night. Finally, around five a.m., I turn the cab in and cash out. Done. I am exhausted, but still wide awake. On the way home, I drive to a vacant lot and park my car.

And I just sit there, staring into the hazy night
    As hellish machines growled in the distance.
What a day.
What a nightmare.
I give thanks to the gods for testing my resolve
    in a manner I couldn't have imagined.
Just as I had marveled at the sun setting
    on the sewage pond earlier in the day,
I then watch the sun rise
As the foggy chord of morning
Twangs into the dawn,
Knowing that soon,
I would clamber
For the mercy of sleep.

DOMESTIC DISPUTE

I pull up. Clothes are spread all over the front yard. I've been given a call to pick up in a residential neighborhood. A man walks out of a house carrying a cardboard box. It's stuffed with various items. Behind him, a woman charges out of a screen door. It claps shut on a spaghetti hinge. She runs up, kicks the man in the ass. He turns and grabs her by the arms. They wrestle in the yard.

I roll down the window and ask if either of them called a cab.

They ignore me and continue wrestling.

I ask again.

No reply.

As I begin to pull away, the man suddenly yells.

"Hold up! I'm coming! Don't leave me here!"

COPS VS. CABS

Since all the cab drivers that work for the cab company drive old cop cars and work the same streets, I naively assumed there'd be some kind of loose camaraderie among the cops and cabdrivers. But I was badly mistaken. The cops don't like us. At all. There is no camaraderie. There is no night shift solidarity between us. From what I've observed, there isn't even any mutual respect, at least from their end. They simply don't like us.

To be fair, there's not much time for any brotherly bonding even if they did like us. Nope. The only way I could describe our relationship is one of begrudging tolerance.

For example, tonight I had a cop pull alongside me while in traffic. He shot me a dirty look. In so many words, his look expressed a very specific message:

"Slow down, scumbag! Don't even think about speeding on my watch!"

I smile and nod.

Just do your job, buddy.

And I'll do mine.

CRAZY FOR JESUS

Call to pick up at a mental health facility. I roll up. Out walks a tall, skinny, long-haired guy, approximately fifty-five years old. He's toting an army bag and a boom box. He informs me that he is getting transferred to another mental facility across town.

Why?

"I'm too nuts for this place."

I nod.

We roll and he launches into a lengthy, Jesus-inspired monologue about life, the end of days, the Bible, and sinful behavior. I listen passively. As far as religious-inspired crazy talk, it's fairly typical and not that interesting. But I don't fault him for it.

If he didn't have something to believe in, what would he have?

He continues to talk, but when he realizes I've lost interest in the conversation, he quiets down. A few minutes later, he sneezes several times in a row. When it's over, I say "God bless you."

His eyes light up as if we are long-lost brothers, and he begins talking about Jesus again.

Dammit.

We pull into the parking lot of his new temporary home: the other mental health facility. I exit the cab and help him unload his duffle bag and boom box. As he prepares himself to leave, a strange, lonely expression appears on his face. We make awkward eye contact.

It's just the two of us here.

No family or friends.

We stand in the parking lot.

Uncomfortable.

Silent for a moment.

I lean over and pat him on the back.

It's going to be alright, buddy.

"You think so?"

Yes, I do.

He reaches out to me for a hug.

And I give him one.

He gets a tear in his eye.

I wish him luck.
I watch him turn and walk toward the mental facility.
For a second there,
He didn't have his Jesus or his religion.
All he had was me.
And I'm not sure if it was enough.

WENDY

12:43 a.m. Call to pick up at the horse track. When I arrive, the place is desolate. Possibly closed. No lights. No crowds. No nothing. As I drive across the giant expanse of the massive parking lot, I see a woman near a car. As I approach, I see that she is being pulled by her arm by someone in the car. They are attempting to drag her into the car.

As I get closer, I recognize the woman. Her name is Wendy. She lives in the same cheap motel where I live. She is one of the local streetwalkers.

I steer the cab toward them, assuming she is the one who called for the cab. It's obvious that something is not right.

I stop and cautiously exit the cab.

I approach them slowly.

The man lets go of her arm.

Wendy runs past me, crying hysterically. She jumps in the back seat of the cab.

The man quickly drives off into the darkness.

I watch him drive away, then I return to the cab.

I put it in gear, and we roll.

She continues to cry.

It's going to be OK, I say.

"That motherfucker was going to kill me."

Sobs.

"You just saved my life."

What the hell was going on?

"He was trying to pull me in the car."

Who is he?

"I don't know."

What did he say?

"I got a bad feeling from him and tried to leave."

We roll in silence.

I stare off into the darkness.

I wonder how long the echo
    of this experience
    will resound
    in the haunted chambers
    of her heart.

XMAS IN RETROGRADE

It's holiday season. The streets are teeming with traffic. Popcorn Christmas lights festoon the houses. Nativity scenes crowd the front yards, but there is no holiday cheer in the collective driving etiquette of humankind during the holidays. The people in traffic all going at it like ruthless maniacs, unfeeling and brutal.

This time of year brings out something cruel in people.

All of the suppressed holiday frustrations are expressed in the theater of five o'clock traffic. No one is thinking about the gentle heart of the sleeping Baby Jesus as they careen, demented and temporarily insane, through yellow lights and congested intersections. In the yuletide maelstrom, I can hear the telepathy of their innermost thoughts as I attempt to merge into oncoming traffic.

"Back off! Ye shall not disrupt nor gain entry to the satanic momentum of my fixed pace!"

Alpha males and housewives in minivans are the most cruel and unforgiving. They enter a realm that few souls can dream of. It is an amoral chamber of power that shows no mercy. They enter a trance-like state of complete and utter domination.

With horrifying precision,
    They hasten to block,
    Brake to taunt,
    Accelerate to defeat,
    And tailgate to conquer.
The tyranny of their souls
    Does not cease
    Until
    The Christmas trees
    Are ash upon the ground
    And the holidays
    Are no longer a weapon
    Used to dehumanize one another
    In the coliseum
    Of traffic.

THE RULES

Here are some things I have learned while driving a cab.

- If the fare is over twenty dollars, always collect it in advance. It weeds out the runners and thieves.
- Avoid the FM radio.
- Instead, listen closely to the CB radio and the dispatcher.
- Hide your money in your shoe or under the seat.
- Keep the cab's doors locked at all times.
- Drive with bright lights on in poorly lit neighborhoods.
- Always trust your gut.
- Keep a crack in the window to monitor sounds in the environment.
- Wait no longer than five minutes at any given address and have the transmission in DRIVE—never locked in PARK.
- Avoid distractions. Know that at any time you could be shot, robbed, or ambushed from any direction by anyone.
- The poorer people are, the harder they dream.

THE TOYLAND BATTLEFIELD MEMORIAL

I pick up three dudes at a country house in Vatican, Louisiana. They're all in their early twenties. They pile into the back seat. They talk stoner gibberish as I drive. They don't seem very smart. I wonder how they survive. How do they get by? How do they support themselves?

We arrive at their destination. It's a shithole apartment complex known as Ile Des Cannes. As we pull up, I see something odd. The parking lot of the apartment complex is littered with hundreds of children's toys. Colorful, broken toys scattered everywhere. Hundreds of them.

It's like a plastic battlefield.
Broken Big Wheels.
Headless baby dolls.
Crumpled Monopoly money.
Disemboweled stuffed animals.
Dead remote-controlled cars.
Discarded building blocks.
Spent Legos like shell casings.

There are so many of these toys lying around, I have to run over them in order to pull into the parking lot. The plastic buckles and pops under the wheels of the cab. The residents of the complex, who are loitering in the late afternoon sun, don't seem to notice me, the toys, or anything.

They don't care.
Why should they?
They just live here.
I watch them.
They stare zombie-like into the distance,
    As if waiting for someone
    Or something
    To come
    And flush it all away.

ASSAULTED BY THE CRACK LADY

Pick up at an auto parts store. I roll up to the address and see an undernourished woman in her forties, standing alone in a sunbaked parking lot. She is involuntarily moving her body around, gesturing wildly at ghosts. I assume she is a crack addict. She hops into the front seat and begins a drug-fueled, rambling monologue. I deduce that she wants to go to a motel up the road.

Quick note: crack addicts are very unpredictable. Every call to pick up a crack addict implies some degree of hassle and the possibility of not getting paid. Many of them use cabs to get around town. So, we deal with them a lot. Sometimes you get paid. Sometimes you just get the hassle.

We roll. Roughly a few minutes into the ride, she asks if we can stop at a friend's house. No. I inform her that I am only obligated to deliver her to her given destination, which is the hotel she requested upon entering the cab. I've already called it into the dispatcher. It's already set. And we're busy. And I have other calls to pick up.

And on that note, without warning or reason, the woman attempts to grab the steering wheel of the cab and force it to the side of the road.

Oh my God.

I push her arms away and wrestle control of the wheel back from her. I warn her not to do it again.

"I'm sorry. I just want to see my friend."

Nope. Sorry. I'm going to drop you off at the motel you requested.

We continue our journey. She quiets down.

But then, as if there is profoundly flawed wiring in her brain, she tries to grab the wheel again. Oh, no you don't! I shove her away from the steering wheel. This really pisses her off. And things deteriorate from there. I pull into a parking lot and bring the cab to halt.

Get out of the cab! I tell her. This ride is over. You're a danger to yourself and everyone on the road.

"Fuck you!"

She refuses to exit the cab.

Pause. Thinking.

I exit the cab and walk around to her side. I open her door. Time to go. I point to the street. With arms folded like a stubborn child, she refuses to leave. Instead, she lunges for the CB radio and begins yelling into the mic.

"Attention! I need help. The cabdriver is trying to hurt me!"

Oh my God.

What the fuck is wrong with you?

I grab her by the arm and attempt to politely pull her out of the cab.

"Don't you touch me!" she screams, LOUDLY.

I don't know what to do.

I think of Dale the old-timer who cautioned me about the dangers of having a crazy woman in your cab. He advised me that the only way to resolve the problem—whatever it may be—was to grab them by the hair and drag them out of the cab. I am embarrassed to admit that this option did gain some traction in my mind for a few minutes. I began to envision and calculate the angle and speed that would be necessary to grab a proper chunk of her hair and pull her out of the cab. But her hair was very thin, discolored, and ragged. Thus, it probably would not possess the structural integrity needed to properly execute this maneuver.

Sigh.

She continues screaming into the radio.

At this point, I can hear the dispatcher actually yelling back at her.

"Ma'am, you need to get off this radio! This is a licensed frequency for cab business only!"

"He's hurting me! He put his hands on me!"

I roll my eyes and back away from her and the cab.

She sits there yelling, cursing. Hysterical. I turn around and walk away to gather myself. Immediately, I hear the sound of slippers hurriedly slapping the pavement behind me. The woman runs up and punches me in the back of the head. I turn around and she backs away.

"Come on, motherfucker!" she screams.

Oh my God.

Can I please just get back to work and have a normal day?

I've already written off this five-dollar fare. There's no way I will get paid by this woman. I just want to go back to work now. I give up. I turn away from her and once again, she runs up and attempts to hit me in the head. This time, I see her coming at me. I jump out of the way and give her a shove her away from me. She trips and goes skidding along the pavement.

Pause.

I realize this is my chance to escape her.

While she's getting off the ground, I run, jump in the cab. I throw it in gear, and I roll out in a cloud of putrid summer dust.

Wheels spinning.

Goodbye, crazy lady.

In the rearview mirror, I see her cursing and gesticulating at me.

"Fuck you! Pussy motherfucker!"

Best of luck out there, ma'am.

She's really pissed off. I imagine she thinks that she is the victim in this situation. That it was I who did her wrong.

Sigh.

I have to keep reminding myself

    That everyone in the modern world

    Imagines themselves the victim.

    It's the one thing we all have in common.

YEAR OF THE KNIFE

In the cab business, there exists a multitude of workplace slang associated with the job. The term "flag" is often bantered about by drivers. What is a flag? A "flag" is someone who hails a cab from the side of the road. In short, they "flag you down." Because of the smaller size of this city and the lower volume of passengers, flags don't happen as often in Lafayette as in bigger, metropolitan cities like New York.

Some flags turn out to be good calls. But in Louisiana, many of them are bad. In short, they are often desperate pleas from desperate people looking to exit a desperate situation. Down here in Louisiana, you don't get flagged by businessmen leaving a board meeting. Instead, you get flagged by people tossed out of cars, kicked out of their apartment, or recently released from jail. They come with a bit more risk, because there is no phone number or data documenting their interaction with you like there is when someone goes through the normal procedure of calling a cab.

It's Sunday. The night shift is slow. People stay home and watch TV, recover from the weekend. As I'm driving along, I see a guy walking on the side of the road. He sees me and flags me down. I debate whether to pick him up. I remind myself that the shift is very slow, and I haven't made much money, so I pull over to hear him out, which turns out to be a lot.

He's a regular-looking dude. 180 lbs. Midthirties. He wants to go to Maurice, Louisiana, roughly thirty minutes away. It's a twenty-five-dollar fare, I tell him. But this guy doesn't have any money. That's not a good sign.

"Money's on the other side," he says. "My father will pay for it."

I shake my head.

"I swear. You'll get your money when we get there."

Sigh.

Fuck it. I decide to take my chances. You take what you can get on slow nights. That's the gamble.

This dude immediately reveals himself to be a piece of work. First off, he talks a lot. Too much, like he is nervous.

That makes me nervous.

Secondly, he's obnoxiously overconfident.

That makes me suspicious.

Sometimes when a passenger has no money, a driver will ask to hold the passenger's ID until payment is made.

"I'm a drug dealer," he says. "I never carry cash or ID on me."

That's weird. And also not a good sign. I should drop the guy off now on the side of the road, but I'm committed. I'm an optimist. Maybe he will have the money. But the farther we get up the road, the more he talks. And the more I realize I made a mistake. The tone of his voice is shaky. He's probably going to run. I should've passed on this one. As we get closer to his destination, which is way out in the country, he grows increasingly anxious. Squirming in his seat. Acting odd.

This fool is going to run on me, I know it. I can feel his nervousness grow. I study him in the rear-view mirror. His demeanor slowly mutates from that of a boastful dude to that of a desperate and sketchy crackhead. As we near the supposed address of his father's house, his directions become increasingly vague.

"Turn left here."

He fidgets with his hands.

"Take a right there."

He rolls down the window and squirms in the seat.

"Now go around the block."

"OK. Slow down."

Finally, he points to a house.

"Don't park in the driveway!"

I pull the cab into the driveway.

"Man, I said don't pull in the driveway!"

Before I can tell him to chill, he bolts out of the cab.

Motherfucker! I knew it. I kick open my door and give chase.

We weave past a fence and go around another house. But I'm right behind him. I catch him by the shoulder, throw my weight forward, and tackle him to the ground.

We begin throwing punches.

He misses.

I punch him in the head a couple times.

He swings at me.

I block it.

I punch him again.

We wrestle around.

I pin him down and hold him there.

Why the fuck did you run? I yell at him.

He begins sobbing.

"Man, I was having a bad night," he pleads. "I'm sorry. I just needed a ride."

Sigh. Unbelievable.

I'm so pissed off, I don't want to hear anything he has to say. I just want to bash his head in.

I recently heard a story about another cabdriver who was shot and killed two months before I started this job. His murder was in the newspapers and a common conversation topic among cabdrivers on slow nights.

The killer shot him in the head and then sat on top of the cabdriver's dead body and drove the cab to a vacant lot where he abandoned it. The cabdriver's name was Clement Pryor. He was a retired tax auditor with the Lafayette Parish School Board. He had only been driving for three weeks. He only took the job to keep busy and earn extra money.

I think about Clement Pryor. I was one of the new hires that replaced him.

I think about all the other cabdrivers who have been ripped off and run on.

I think about how I will have to pay for this guy's fare at the end of the night.

I remember that I have a knife in my pocket.

I stare down at him, boiling with anger.

I think about lying in my motel room. No money and needing a job.

Then an odd feeling comes over me. I see how scared the guy is. What the fuck am I doing? Why do I want to hurt this dude? It's only a twenty-five-dollar fare. Do I really want to hurt this guy for twenty-five dollars? It's just money. It's not life.

I think about all of us humans fighting and bashing the shit out of each other over money.

It's only money.

Just paper.

I could call the cops. But it would probably take an hour for them to get out here. What am I going to do? Hold this guy down for an hour?

The night is pitch-black and silent.

It's not worth it.

I hear a voice in my head talking louder.

Why do you want to hurt him?

Just let him go.

It's only money.

Who gives a fuck?

Just let him go.

Just let him go.

I loosen my grip.

I take my weight off of him.
And I just let him go.
There's no other way.
There's nothing else to do here.
I tell him to start running.
And he does.
I watch him sprint into the night
    Like a child
    Lost and lonely
    In this world.

Chapter 2
TRAILERVILLE

TRAILERVILLE

After a year of living in motels, I had to get out. It was an interesting experiment, but its time had come to an end. I got tired of the night crawlers and drug addicts, lounging around, knocking on my door at all hours of the night, bumming cigarettes, loose change, and whatever else. I just got tired. They wear you out after a while, because you have to keep an eye on them. They'll steal your shit: cell phone, wallet, car, whatever. Doesn't matter.

It was time for a change, so I saved some money and rented a cheap trailer in a country trailer park on the west side of town. It's peaceful here. I call it Trailerville. I think I'm going to like it. And the rent is unbelievably cheap: $225/month. That's cheaper than the motels, and there are a lot less crackheads. The exceptionally cheap rent is partly due to the fact that my trailer was damaged two years ago in Hurricane Lili. It flipped over in high winds. After being put upright, the trailer was never properly leveled, so the whole thing sits at an odd angle like a listing ship. It's not too noticeable unless I'm taking a bath and the water spills out of one side of the tub. Other than that, it's great. Most of the people who live here are kind of kooky, but they're tolerable.

And it's quiet.

And it's not far from the cabstand.

And I still have my job.

Thus, I now begin my second year

As a cabdriver.

THE ONE-ARMED MAN, PT. 2

Call to pick up at shithole bar. I arrive. Honk. Out comes the One-Armed Man. This guy again. Yes, he's a regular. This is my second time picking him up. He does not remember me from our first encounter. It's closing time and he's wasted, again.

This is what he does:

Drinks excessively until the bar is closed.

And then goes home in a cab.

He approaches the cab and awkwardly tugs open the door. He sits in the front. He likes to sit in the front.

Where to?

"Home."

He gives me his address.

As mentioned previously, he is missing an arm. If I had to speculate on how he lost that arm, I'd say it was a drunk-driving accident—probably sometime in the late 1980s or early '90s. Tonight, he is especially drunk and, as usual, his haircut is highly manicured. It's a near-perfect geodesic dome of aerosol and game show host-like hair. The One-Armed Man's hair does not move. I think I'm more intrigued by the specter of his hair than his missing arm. His hair is regal and grandiose and oddly commanding. Like Beethoven at the mall.

We roll.

"You smoke weed?" he asks.

No.

"You do coke?" he asks.

Nope.

"You drink?"

Socially, I reply.

"You're no fun," he sniffs.

We arrive at his house.

I pull up parallel to his yard at the walkway that leads to his front door.

He pays the fare.

As he gathers himself up and steps out the cab, he promptly tumbles straight into the ditch in front of his house. He just disappears, like a ship lost in the Bermuda Triangle of his yard.

I step out of the cab.

Walk around.

There he is, lying in the ditch.

Flat on his back.

Face up.

Staring at the sky.

In his one hand, he holds a pack of rolling papers and a partially burning cigarette lodged between his fingers.

"Just leave me here," he says. "I'll be fine."

No, I'll help you get up, I reply. We have to get you up and in the house.

"No, no, I'm all right."

Let me help you up.

As I stare down at him, I notice smoke wafting off of his head.

"Leave me alone."

I look closer.

On the crown of his highly manicured haircut, I see the burning embers of his cigarette.

The cherry, dislodged and burning in his hair.

It is still lit and smoking.

I laugh out loud and swat the cherry out of his hair.

Like a bug.

"Leave me alone!"

I grab him by his one arm and attempt to pull him to his feet. But he resists my attempts. Instead, he lazily reclines back into the ditch.

I try to pull him up again.

"Leave me alone!" he yells, again. "I just want to stay here!"

OK. I back off.

Stare at him.

I assess the situation.

Look around.

He lives in a nice, safe neighborhood.

There is no danger.

So, I guess he'll be alright.

He'll probably pass out and wake in an hour.

And then go inside.

With clear conscience, I decide to leave him to his lot.

I'm leaving, I tell him.

He gives me a lazy, stoned salute.

I climb in the cab

And leave him there
In the ditch
To marvel at the miracle of life
And its many manifestations
And to contemplate his place
In the rightful order of things.

A MAN CALLED FISH

Typical night. I pick up two rednecks carrying a twelve-pack of beer. Where are they going? Travel Lodge Hotel. It's a low-rent dive. Got it.

We roll.

"Can we stop at a store?"

Yes.

We stop at a nearby gas station. They pick up another twelve-pack of beer. I make polite conversation with the redneck up front. He's wearing a fishing hat.

"They call me Fish!"

OK. Nice to meet you, Fish.

Fish is abrasive and loud, and he asks dumb questions.

"You can't drive any faster than this?"

"Can you get us some whores?"

"Where are you from?"

I just ignore him. He doesn't like that. He mumbles under his breath. Fish is a certified asshole. I'm not sure if they're born or made, but there are a lot of them out there. And according to my calculations and experiences in the cab, they're not going away any time soon. In fact, they're probably taking over. We pull up to their motel. It's Friday night. Everyone is off work. Lots of people hanging in the parking lot: young laborers, dope dealers and addicts, random drifters. I stop the cab in the center parking lot. Put it in PARK.

I turn to Fish and tell him the fare: seven dollars.

Fish bristles.

"Seven dollars? Fuck that!"

I sigh. Fish eyeballs me hard. We begin having an undeclared staring contest. Just looking at one another. In the eyes. It gets tense in the cab very quickly.

"Let's go!" says Fish

He motions for me to step outside the cab and fight.

Sounds like a great idea.

We both step out of the cab.

He puts his twelve-pack down and curses at me.

Within minutes, we're surrounded by a crowd of listless motel denizens and drifters. They want to see some action. People love a fight. Absolutely love it. They love violence.

Fish is stocky. I step toward him. I really want to ring his bell. Just one good punch in the jaw. We circle one another. Fish scrambles around, antsy, talks some more shit.

"He's got a knife!" he screams, pointing at me.

I look around, confused. I don't have a knife. I don't know who or what he's talking about. Fish is full of shit.

"He's got a knife!

Fish calls out to his friend.

"Billy give me your knife!"

Billy just stands there.

"That motherfucker's got a knife, I'm telling you!"

We stand there with our fists in the air.

Fish. What an asshole.

I kind of wish I had a knife.

I shake my head wondering what'll happen next.

I hear the dispatcher call me on the CB radio.

"Driver Four, where are you?"

I ignore it.

Fish looks at me. Then looks back at the cab. I realize Fish really doesn't want to fight. He just wants to talk shit in front of his buddies.

I walk toward the cab. As I do, Fish suddenly gets courageous. He bangs on the hood of the cab. I run toward him. Fish runs away, backing up.

Cat and mouse.

I charge and swing at him. My fist connects with the side of his head. Fish stumbles and trips.

The motel people yell and holler.

"That white boy punched that dude upside his head!"

"I'm telling you, he's got a knife!"

I don't have a knife, you asshole! Just pay the fare and I'll go.

"I ain't paying for shit!"

It's only seven dollars, Fish!

"No way!"

I'm over it. I have better things to do than dick around with Fish. I cut my losses and jump back in the cab. Fish cusses at me from a safe distance. I wave goodbye to everyone.

God bless the American Wasteland! I scream.

I return to the shift, picking up the next set of calls. Thirty minutes later, the dispatcher calls me on the radio.

"Driver Four, I just got a complaint from some guy at that hotel where you just dropped off."

Roll my eyes.

Yeah, what's up with them?

"He says you pulled a knife on him," says the dispatcher. "Is that true?"

Sigh.

Of course not! Did he happen to mention that he didn't pay their fare?

"No, he didn't."

I didn't think so.

"He wants to file a complaint."

Tell him to file whatever he wants.

"Copy that."

Fucking Fish.

What an asshole.

TIBB

1:43 a.m. Nearing closing time at the bars. During closing time, we get a lot of calls from bartenders, trying to flush out the last of the drunk customers. These would be the customers that are too drunk to safely drive home. Tonight, I get a call to pick up at Wranglers Bar in Carencro, Louisiana. I pull up. Honk. Wait. No one comes out. I park, kill the cab, walk in the bar, and locate the bartender.

Who called for the cab?

Bartender points to the end of the bar. There's a sixty-something-year-old Cajun man slumped on his bar stool. Drooling.

"He's very drunk," warns the bartender.

I walk over, tap the guy on the shoulder.

I'm your cabdriver. I'm going to take you home.

He turns and looks at me.

"I'm Tibb, dammit! Thib-bo-deaux!"

I nod.

Sounds good.

He rises off of the bar stool and begins stumbling his way out of the bar. I shadow him to make sure he doesn't fall, occasionally grabbing him by the arm. He sways. Trips. Knocks over someone's drink. Apologizes. As we exit the bar, we navigate past a leisurely drunken crowd gathered outside. Tibb suddenly decides he doesn't need my help anymore. He shakes his arm loose.

"I can walk on my own, goddammit!"

OK.

Tibb wobbles about in the parking lot. Tilts at odd angles between cars. He leans hard left, then hard right. Picks up speed. Tries to catch his balance. And then goes down in heap. I lean over to help him up. But now, he's so fucking drunk, he thinks somebody hit him.

He grabs my shirt.

"Who are you, motherfucker?!"

I calmly remind him that I am his cabdriver, and that I'm here to help him get home safely.

"I'm Tibb, dammit! Get your fucking hands off me!"

Sigh.

OK, Tibb. You're on your own.

Drunk people are like kids, but way more annoying.

Come on, Tibb. Let's get out of here, buddy.

I help him up. Some people cheer and laugh.

"Go home!" someone yells.

We pass a guy selling burgers in the parking lot.

"Somebody buy me a hamburger," yells Tibb to no one in particular.

As I'm trying to get Tibb in the cab, a burger magically appears. Someone hands it to Tibb.

But Tibb doesn't want it now. He throws it at a parked car. The people laugh.

"I got to piss!" Tibb announces.

I shake my head. Tibb leans sideways against the cab to steady himself. He pulls out his dick and sprays piss everywhere like a fountain. Urine dances in circles down his pants and on a nearby parked car. He's a mess. I look around. Nobody cares. They're too drunk, eating hamburgers.

I finally get Tibb in the cab. We roll.

Tibb begins to randomly announce things at high volume.

"I've been living here seventy-two years!"

We weave through traffic.

"Everybody knows Tibb!"

He spits out the window and points: "I was born in that house!"

Farther up the road: "That motherfucker still owes me money!"

We finally arrive at his house. I pull into Tibb's driveway. He pays the fare. No arguments. I try to help him get out.

"I don't need no help!"

No problem.

"I brought myself up into this world. I can get myself home."

You're a big boy now, Tibb.

"I sure as hell am!"

Tibb exits the cab

    Takes a few steps

        Stumbles

    Recovers

        Steadies himself

    Reaches down

        And then pulls out his penis again

        And urinates in his front yard.

"I'm Tibb!" he screams out into the universe.

You sure as hell are, buddy.

I wave goodbye and roll out of there,
    Watching Tibb
    As he sways in the yard
    Pissing away his demons.

SCENES FROM HURRICANE KATRINA

On August 29, 2005, Hurricane Katrina made landfall in southern Louisiana.

Here are some of the scenes I witnessed:

- semi-martial law in downtown Baton Rouge
- buses and supply trucks, moving 100 mph down I-10, evacuating people from New Orleans
- two guys dressed in prison garb, who claimed their clothes had "blown off" in the storm and the local jail gave them orange jump-suits
- no hotel vacancies for five hundred miles
- people sleeping in their cars at Walmart
- people sleeping in tents outside of churches
- roving packs of people in Baton Rouge, just walking the streets
- a New Orleans cabbie who had been living in his cab for a week
- hundreds of people stranded at the Greyhound Bus station
- two guys who paddled a canoe around New Orleans for two days and finally got out
- dozens of abandoned cars along I-10

THE WALLET

I pick up a guy at Greyhound station. Midforties, tall, lanky. He struts up to the cab and climbs in.

Where to?

"Carencro."

He gives me the address of a trailer park.

"I hate this fucking place."

Which place are you talking about?

"This place. This whole town," he says. "Country-ass towns."

He's a Katrina evacuee. There's a lot of them living here now. They've got nowhere else to go. This guy is a piece of work. He bitches and moans a lot: Lafayette, FEMA, the cab, the fare, the women, the men, the food.

He gives me a lot of bad attitude the whole way.

"You sound like you're in a bad mood."

I was just about to tell you the same.

He lets out a disgusted half-chuckle. "If only yawl motherfuckers knew how bad a mood I done been in."

I nod. Granted, I feel really bad for the victims of the hurricane. They deserve a lot of sympathy, but this guy's just an asshole, trying to lay his burden on everyone else.

"I don't give a fuck. I always bounce back."

I hope you do, buddy.

We arrive at his trailer park. I ask him which trailer is his. He doesn't reply. I turn around and ask again. Where's your trailer?

"Number thirty-four, man!" he yells.

I shake my head and locate his trailer. He pays the fare. He offers no thanks and no tip. Just silence. I watch him lazily strut through the cold darkness of October toward his trailer. Stone-cold Mr. Cool. Strutting for no one and nothing. There's literally no one around but him and me to witness this regal display of attitude. But he's still fronting it like he's on the red carpet. Maybe that's how he copes with it—the stress and whatnot.

I roll out of there.

About three miles up the road, the dispatcher calls me on the radio.

"That guy you just dropped off. He thinks he left his wallet in your cab."

OK. What do you want me to do?

"Can you look around for it?"

Sure.

I pull over and turn on the interior light. I feel around and find it wedged in the back seat. It's a black Velcro wallet—the kind you buy when you're fifteen. I grab it and toss it next to me on the seat.

I radio the dispatcher. Tell him I found it.

"Can you drive back there and drop it off to him?"

10-4.

I swing the cab around and backtrack to the trailer park. Halfway there, I start to wonder about what's in his wallet. I'm not the kind of person who would go through other people's shit, but this guy was such an asshole, I think, why not? I grab the wallet and then I put it back down. Think twice. Then I pick it up again. Keep driving. Repeat. Fuck it. I pull over. I grab the wallet. I look inside. It's stuffed with debit and credit cards, a FEMA card, his driver's license, some business cards, phone numbers, six dollars in cash, and lastly, a dime bag of weed.

I close the wallet and throw it back on the seat. I immediately feel like an asshole. But I doubt I'll lose much sleep over it. I pull up to his trailer. Honk. It's 12:20 a.m. He doesn't come out. Honk again. Still no sign. I guess this asshole expects me to hand-deliver his Velcro wallet. Right to his busted-ass doorstep. I roll my eyes, grab the wallet, and exit. I knock on his door. I can hear a TV blaring inside, so I knock twice more. Hard. He jerks open the door. Stands there. Staring. His entire body language reeks of insolence even more so than before, if that's possible.

"Wassup?" he says.

What do you think's up? I got your wallet. The one you forgot in the cab.

I toss it to him. He opens it and checks the contents. As he does this, I notice he is chewing on some kind of orange mush. It looks like orange tapioca pudding. Whatever it is, it's gross. I can see it in his mouth. He's smacking on it. Loudly. What the hell is up with that? Even his smacking is cocky.

"Everything better be in here," he says. "Or I'll have to kill you."

I shake my head.

Is that right?

Good luck, motherfucker.

I can't believe this asshole. What a turd. I turn and walk toward the cab. Once again, no thanks. And no tip. No nothing.

I should've stolen his fucking weed.

THE FUR HAT

The dispatcher calls.

"Pick up a lady in Grand Coteau," he says. "She's wearing a fur hat."

A what?

"A fur hat. She's in a parking lot."

Where at?

"At the Chase Bank."

And she's got a fur hat?

"10-4."

I look up the address and roll. When I arrive, I pull into the area described and see a cute little old lady waiting under a tree. And indeed, she is wearing a Russian-like fur hat with Ignatius J. Reilly flaps. I beep the horn and wave. She waves back and hops in.

Where do you want to go?

"The Motel 6," she says. "I'm a FEMA person." She speaks with what sounds like an Italian accent.

What's a FEMA person?

"My house was destroyed in the hurricane. I've been living hotels for three months. I hate these hotels! Now, please, drive me back to the hotel."

We roll. She's looks about sixty-five years old.

"I lost my IDs and my green cards. I lost everything in the flood!" She gazes out of the window and speaks uninterrupted.

"You are nice man. But drive too fast."

She talks about her health, her doctor, her dog, her old house, and the storm. But more than anything, she talks about her dead husband.

"He was a beautiful man."

How did he pass away?

"His brother beat him to death. That son of a bitch! He killed him with his hands! Beat him. With his hands. My husband worked for Governor Edwards. Good governor. He was a real estate assessor. His brother was jealous of him. Jealous of his money. He beat him dead!"

She goes silent.

I peek at her in the mirror.

She's crying

    Beneath the cloak

    Of her fur hat.

THE DEAF MUTES

Pick up: grocery store. I roll up and see two middle-aged women and a young girl waiting for me. They have three carts of groceries. I hop out to assist in loading them in the trunk. One of them hands me a business card.

It has the following written on it.

> *We are deaf-mute and on Social Security.*
> *Can you please help us with our groceries?*
> *Our address is: 232 Simon Dr. Lafayette, LA*
> *Thank you & God Bless*

I nod and give a thumbs up.

The two women have short haircuts cut in the style sometimes preferred by lesbians in the 1980s. As I'm loading their groceries in the trunk, the little girl leans over to me.

"Sir, can you please pick up your pants? I can see your butt crack."

AND THE BLIND SHALL PUKE

Call to pick up at Bisbano's Pizza. I arrive and honk. No one comes out. The dispatcher asks me to go inside and check on them.

"The customers are blind. You might have to help them."

10-4.

I park and walk into the establishment. I quickly locate the customers at a booth: a young man and woman, both in their twenties. They have folding canes and are indeed blind. In addition, they are both drunk. Several empty pitchers of beer sit in front of them.

"It's my birthday," says the young woman.

They have been celebrating. We exit the bar. Behind me, they drunkenly tap their canes on the pavement, feeling their way to the cab. I don't know what to do, so I lead them with my voice.

This way.

Keep coming.

Over here.

A little to the right.

They slowly climb into the cab.

Where to?

"My apartment."

She tells me the address. We roll. I drive like I usually do, which is fast. They sit in the back seat, talking, mumbling, sometimes grunting. After cutting through a busy intersection and darting around a few slower cars, I hear a gurgling sound in the back seat. Out of the corner of my eye, I see an explosion of white puke spray across the rear of the cab.

Oh, shit.

The girl is puking in the cab. It looks like oatmeal and beer. I hastily steer the cab into a parking lot. Upon stopping, I hop out. Walk around and open her door. She leans her head out and pukes on the ground. The blind guy sits there, listening. He's got puke on his pants. He stares into the void of this life, his face expressionless. She pukes two more times. Then we roll on. I tell her if she needs to puke again to let me know and I'll pull over.

"Can you drive slower?" she asks.

YES.

They both nod.

We arrive at their apartment with no more puking episodes. They assemble their canes and exit the cab. She hands me her keys.

"Can you open my apartment door?"

Yes.

I hop out, run to her door. Open it. It's a strange sight to watch, drunk blind people swaying, tapping their canes, and trying to remain upright. Once again, I lead them with my voice.

This way.

Come on.

Keep it coming.

You're almost there.

It takes them a few minutes, but they make it to the apartment.

I realize that I need to clean the cab. Inside their apartment, I locate some paper towels in a cupboard and run back to the cab. I wipe up the puke and clean the seats and floor. Completing that task, I walk back into their apartment and wash my hands.

As I'm leaving, I notice the place is completely dark, so I click on a light. They're both passed out on the couch. Then I remember they are blind, so I turn off the light and quietly close the door. I wonder if this is a sign of the apocalypse. Like a biblical, Revelations thing:

And the blind shall become drunk
and puke upon themselves
the pizzas and beers
which they have consumed
as the serpents rain down from the sky . . .

I let myself out of the apartment,
    Hoping the blind
        Will sleep peacefully tonight.

HEARTSTRINGS

I am parked in the ghetto,
Waiting for the next call
When I see a homeless man
Sitting on a curb
Across the street.
He sips from a beer in a bag.
He's oblivious to everyone.
I watch him for a few minutes,
Just observing him.
Then all of sudden,
I feel a string section swell in my heart
And I see the decades of pain
Ripple across his face.
I get a distant sense of the huge sadness
That has probably plagued him
For his entire life.
It's a symphony of sadness
That has spat him out
Here
Onto this curb
Where I watch him.
     The heart is a funny thing.
     It sneaks up on you
     When you aren't ready.

THE PENTACOSTAL PARTY TRAIN

Pick up: Holiday Inn. Passengers: two chicks and one gay guy. One of them is turning twenty-five. So, they're celebrating. They are Holiness Apostolic Pentecostals from Krotz Springs, Louisiana. They are nice and chatty.

"It's the most hardcore of the Pentecostals," one of them volunteers.

Last year, they all left the church. Lost their religion.

Why? I ask.

"Because it's fucked."

They grew up dirt poor. Eight brothers and sisters. No birth control.

"Where do people go here for fun?"

Bars. Clubs.

"Can you take us to a big party club?"

Yes.

From the tone of their conversation, it's obvious they are very sweet, good-natured people. I find them mildly fascinating. One of the girls tells a story about getting gangbanged while her cousins were in the next room.

"I liked it," she says.

One of the male participants was a sixteen-year-old virgin, she tells me.

Wow. When the screw turns, it really turns.

The other girl tells me she married a cop but divorced him after two years.

Why?

"He was nuts. Totally paranoid," she says. "I couldn't go anywhere. He didn't want me to leave the house or do anything."

The gay guy talks about being completely alienated from his family, friends, and church for being gay. I bet that's a rough ride, growing up gay in small-town Louisiana.

"The repression in the church was really bad," he says. "Anytime you repress sex, people get weird."

No argument there. The conversation dies off.

I drop them at the big party club in town where people go to drink and dance. When they see all the people waiting in line to get in the club, they get excited.

"Yes. This is going to be cool!"

I guess they're still playing catch up.

Have fun, I say.

I roll out.

Four hours later, they call for me to pick them up. I drive back to the club and locate them near the entrance.

Did you have fun?

"We had a blast."

What'd you do?

"Danced and talked to sleazy old guys."

How was that?

"They bought us a lot of drinks."

I drive them back to the Holiday Inn. They're only slightly drunk. Not bad for rookies. They're so innocent and friendly. I kind of feel sad for them. I don't know why, something about them. They resonate a unique sorrow, they're very genuine. I don't know how to properly describe it. They believed in something. And now they don't. And that seems sad.

I drop them off at the hotel. I don't charge them for the cab ride. This one is on me.

"Thank you so much!"

It feels wrong to take money from them. I don't know why. They give me hugs and say goodnight. And then they disappear into the party of their lives.

QUEST FOR LOVE

Tuesday night, 2:20 a.m. Call to pick up at a strip club. My passenger is a guy named Doobie, who tells me he's Haitian. He's also frustrated.

"I spent $130 on a dancer in there. And then she rolled out on me."

Sometimes things don't work out.

"She split out the back of the club."

I nod. I guess he thought his $130 was going to buy him some extra benefits.

Doobie leans toward me and says, "I got to get laid."

Is that right?

"Can you find me a girl?" he asks.

I shrug. I don't know. Maybe. It's a Tuesday night, though.

Not much going on.

I've quickly learned that finding men prostitutes is a regular part of this cab job. The protocol is to drive them around parts of town where prostitutes walk the streets. When you see one, you pull over, roll down the window, and let the customer negotiate what they want. If they come to an agreement, you drive them to a motel, apartment, or house to do their business. It's all part of the night shift.

Most streetwalkers are drug addicts. I inform Doobie of this.

You sure you want to do this?

"Yes, let's go."

We roll out and hit a few of the spots where the streetwalkers hang out.

It's a slow Tuesday night. Odds aren't great that many girls will be out. In fact, after trolling the streets for half an hour, we see zero girls.

Not looking good, buddy.

We head down Carmel Drive and a few other spots, but don't see anyone.

Then I see a dude named Creole Joe.

He's a drug addict and street hustler. And he still owes me money from a previous unpaid cab ride. Joe pops up every six months, in between stints in jail. Because he is a drug addict, he knows a lot of prostitutes. I pull the cab alongside him.

Hey.

"What's up, man?!"

I remind him that he owes me.

"I'm gonna get it to you soon."

Where are the girls tonight? I ask.

He perks up.

"Y'all looking? I'll show you."

He hops in the cab and directs us down a few dimly lit sections of his neighborhood. Searching the shadows, we turn a corner and see a skinny woman walking down the street.

"That's her!" says Joe.

We pull up. She's a fucking wreck. Ragged. Missing teeth. Cracked out. Joe hollers at her.

"Hey, girl. You want some work?"

She approaches the cab. She and Joe negotiate the deal, while Doobie looks at me quizzically. Like I have the answers.

"What do you think? Should I go with her?"

I tell him the truth. Absolutely not, I say.

Doobie tells Joe no and we roll on. Creole Joe is now aggravated with me.

"Why'd you tell him that?"

Shut the fuck up, Joe. He's my passenger. I'm looking out for him. If you don't like it get the fuck out of the cab.

Silence.

We roll and continue the search. The streets are desolate. Nothing. Nowhere. We don't find anything. Creole Joe tries to convince Doobie to come to his house where he will call some girls.

"I'll make this shit happen."

No doubt Creole Joe is out to hustle Doobie for whatever money he has left. That's a fact. On the streets, nobody does anything for free. At all.

Since I started driving a cab, I've seen a lot of questionable shit. Too many episodes of desperate people and ruthless behavior. There are no favors. The streets ain't no joke. If you're innocent to the ways of the street, they will run game on your ass and take you for everything they can.

"What should I do?" Doobie asks me.

I shake my head and tell him it's not a good idea.

"Shit, man! Come on," says Joe.

Doobie sits and thinks. He desperately wants to get laid.

"I'm going to go with Joe."

I shrug my shoulders and wish him luck.

On that note, he pays the fare. Creole Joe and Doobie exit the cab. And that's the last I see of them as they disappear into the dark.

I tried to warn him. But everyone's got their own lessons to learn.

Or maybe not.

OLD MAN'S BALLS

The dispatcher gives me a delivery call. We do these on occasion. A delivery call is when a customer calls the cab company and asks us to pick up something and deliver it to an address. Typically, these are small items from a store. The driver goes to the store, buys the item, and delivers it to the customer. The customer reimburses the driver for the cost of the item and price of the fare, which is usually the same cost as a regular cab ride.

The typical items to be delivered include beer, food, and over-the-counter drugs. Delivery calls are annoying, because they slow your workflow and the delivery customers rarely tip. Also, they often request odd things that are hard to locate in a store, such as off-brand, cheap beer or a can of candied yams. It's never Budweiser or Coors. It's always "Bud Ice Light" or something along those lines.

The dispatcher calls me on the radio:

"Pick up a twelve-pack of Keystone Light and a bag of boiled peanuts."

I nod and write it down.

Where to?

"Bring it to 501 Zim Circle."

10-4.

It's always something wacky. I roll to the nearest store and purchase the items. Then I roll to the address, which is located in what is known as the "old people projects." There are a lot of different kinds of projects: crazy people projects, handicapped projects, ghetto projects, the good projects, the bad projects. All kinds of projects. The old people projects are where lower-income senior citizens live. They're pretty mellow. And the old people are usually very nice. I locate the house. Knock on the door. I hear feet shuffling and a TV.

An old man dressed only in a dirty T-shirt opens the door. He's hunched over and smiling.

He's happy I'm here.

"Right on time!"

I hand him the bag and notice his dick and balls are swinging around in his torn boxer underwear. I look the other way.

He gives me the money. I give him his change.

No man should ever have to see

    An old man's balls,

    Or any man's balls for that matter.

    End of story.

BUBBA & THE WHEELCHAIR LADY

Pick up: Best Western Hotel. My passengers are a redneck guy and an older lady in a wheelchair. They are together. I think she is his girlfriend. His name is Bubba. I'll refer to her as the Wheelchair Lady.

Where to?

"How much does it cost to rent this cab for an hour?"

Forty dollars. Anywhere in the city.

"OK. You got it. I got errands to run."

They climb in and we're off on a little adventure with Bubba and the Wheelchair Lady. I load the wheelchair in the trunk. Wheelchair Lady sits in the back seat. Bubba rides up front with me. Bubba calls out the addresses.

"I got business to tend to."

What kind?

"The money kind."

OK.

We roll. Bubba directs me to various neighborhoods. We stop at half a dozen different houses. Bubba goes in. Wheelchair Lady and I wait in the cab. Bubba comes out, counting money. It soon becomes obvious that Bubba is some kind of drug dealer, possibly prescription pills.

We continue to roll. South Side, North Side, Carencro. We stop at a trailer park in Scott. As we're waiting outside for Bubba, three cars pull up. At first, I think they're cops, but then I realize it's a bunch of pillheads who've materialized out of the ether. Bubba comes out and they all perk up. He does his business in the yard, handing out fistfuls of what I assume are pills.

We roll on. Next stop: we head down a gravel road on the outskirts of town. Long road, full of holes. Wheelchair Lady begins to get carsick.

"Can you pull over?"

I stop the cab and give her a breather.

You OK?

"I think so."

We roll on, bouncing down the same road. Dust, gravel, potholes. It goes on for a few miles. The road ends at a barn, and I pull up.

"Pop the horn," says Bubba.

Two guys in cowboy hats appear from the barn. Bubba exits, greets them. They all go into the barn. Cowboy junkies, I think. It's a world full of junkies.

Everyone is addicted to something. Gambling, sex, drugs, work, whatever. Bubba returns and climbs into the cab.

Where to next? I ask.

"Our business is done."

I nod and drive them back to their hotel. As we're driving, he pulls out a huge wad of cash and counts it in his lap.

He hands me forty dollars, tips me another ten dollars.

"Good doing business with you."

ROLL CALL

Tonight's passengers:

- medical package delivery
- KFC worker going home
- two Norwegian oilfield workers
- five Indian students going to Walmart
- yuppie couple going to a restaurant
- woman wearing strange shirt with patches
- chef lady
- Iraq vet
- talkative crackhead
- two carwash employees leaving work
- Honduran man and woman
- dressy couple going to downtown club
- doctor
- thug looking for a job
- kids going to a skating rink
- guy with the flu
- drunk redneck
- drunk salesman
- Asian woman with dog
- guy from Miami going to trucking school

INTO THE NIGHT

It's a long and meditative shift.
Not much action.
As I work
And drive,
I think
Maybe the earth is just a cell farm
For a higher race of beings
And we are just like the ants,
Small, busy, and oblivious.
That is how I feel tonight.
God has disappeared
And so have the forgotten saints,
Now replaced with brutal machines
That grind and spit venomous smoke
Into the sky.
The only prayers left
To say
Are spoken in code
And
In secret,
Hoping
For something
That simply
Is not there.

MOONWALK

First call of the day: a doctor's office in River Ranch. It's in an affluent part of town. I am picking up a blood sample for delivery to a medical lab.

I walk in. There's a guy in the waiting room. He gives me a strange look. I don't know why. Maybe I look crazy.

I see him eyeing me suspiciously, gazing over his newspaper. Perhaps he thinks I would rob him. Who knows?

The receptionist hands me the sample. I turn and moonwalk across the waiting room and out of the door.

THE WIFE'S PANTIES

Pick up: a trailer park. My passenger is an attractive blonde woman. Her destination: a hotel in New Iberia.

"I'm going to meet my husband."

That's nice.

"We're separated. He's on methadone."

OK.

"He just got out of rehab."

OK.

"He's lost his job."

Got you.

"My car is broken right now."

That sucks.

"We have three kids together."

She is curvy and flirtatious. She touches my arm several times during the drive. I try to keep my mind on the road. We arrive at the hotel. The husband walks out to meet us. I grab her suitcases out of the trunk. As I lay them on the ground, one of the suitcases pops open. Panties and sexy lingerie spill on the ground. Embarrassed, I nervously try to scoop them back into the suitcase.

Sorry, I say.

The husband looks at me strangely.

"You trying to get in my wife's panties?"

That's a good one, buddy.

That's funny.

HOW TO FRY CHICKEN

Pick up at Kentucky Fried Chicken. My passenger is an employee who works there. He just finished his shift. He's in a nasty mood and being rude. He complains about my driving.

"You drive too fast."

Then he complains about the temperature in the cab.

"It's hot in here."

Then he accuses me of being rude.

"You must be having a bad night."

People love to complain.

Lastly, he complains about my route to his destination.

"Why are you going this way?"

I turn and tell him:

Dude, don't tell me how to drive

And I won't tell you how to fry chicken.

THE YUPPIE

I'm dispatched to pick up at a fancy bar. My passenger is in his mid-forties. Male. He appears drunk. He's going home. He sits in the back. His address is a rich neighborhood outside of town called Le Triomphe. It has its own golf course and country club. This guy seems aggravated. I ask what is bothering him.

"It's a woman, and it's a long story."

No problem.

We roll on. Ten minutes into the ride, things get quiet. I scan the rear-view mirror and see his head wobble and dip. I turn around. Yes, he is passing out in the back seat of my cab. I give the steering wheel a good shake and tug to jostle him up and around, keep him awake. It works.

You can't let customers pass out. If they pass out, it's highly likely you will not get paid. They are hard to wake when drunk and you cannot take money from their pockets while they are knocked out drunk in the back of your cab. That would be unethical. So, you have to keep them awake. By any means.

We spend most of the twenty-mile drive doing this shake-and-wake ritual, with me tugging the steering wheel every time he starts to pass out. In addition, I turn up the radio and occasionally yell WAKE UP!

"I'm good! I'm up. Just resting my eyes," he says.

Right. OK. Just don't pass out, please.

I ask if he can pay me first, just in case he does pass out. Surprisingly, he agrees and pays me the fare up front, which is considerate. As we're driving, I get a call on my cell phone from a friend. I take the call, which lasts about five minutes. During that time, I lose my focus on the passenger. When the call is complete, I turn to check on the yuppie. And, of course, he passed out and is now sprawled across the seat.

Fuck. I knew it. I knew he'd pass out. I shake my head.

When we get to the guard station at his gated community, I point at the body in the back seat. The security guard gives me a knowing nod and waves me through. I locate the guy's address. It's a big house. Two stories. Long driveway.

How am I going to do this? This guy is passed out. He might not wake.

Halfway up the driveway, I turn the wheel and pull the cab straight onto his lawn. I try to get as close as possible to his front door.

I kill the ignition, walk around to the back of the cab, open his door. I try to wake him. I shake him. Then I bounce the seat up and down a few times. He is not waking. He is drooling. The guy is out cold.

I grab his arms and pull him out of the cab and onto the lawn. He's not a big guy, so this is doable. But it's November and it's cold.

I pause to think.

I can't leave him passed out on his lawn. So, I drag his body toward the house and prop it against the front door. The door is locked, and I don't want him to freeze. The garage door is open, so I search it for a blanket or something. I find some plastic sheeting draped over a riding lawnmower. I grab it, drag it out, and drape it over him. Then I tuck it in around him like a little yuppie baby. I step back, assess the scene.

I am my brother's keeper.

He looks dead. But he is not.
He's just living the high life
    and paying his dues
        like many others
        who have come before him
        and lived to tell the tale.

THE STALKER

I'm downtown waiting on a call when a man in his late forties flags me down near the Greyhound station. He hops in the cab. Front seat. Immediately, I sense something is not right with him.

Where to?

"Have you seen my wife?"

Uh, no.

"She just got in a cab. Did you hear her call on the radio?"

No, I didn't hear anything, my man.

"I know you heard it! My wife and I just got in an argument and I need to find her. I'll pay you twenty dollars!"

He pulls out a roll of bills.

I tell him the truth. I didn't hear the call and even if I did, it's against the law to divulge that information.

"I KNOW YOU KNOW WHERE SHE'S GOING!"

Oh, man. This is too much.

Please just get out of my cab, I tell him.

I've got other calls to pick up. It's a busy night and I don't know where his wife is.

"Can I ride with you for a bit and smoke?"

He makes a weird smoking gesture with his hands, as if holding an imaginary crack pipe.

Smoke what? Crack? In the cab? Absolutely NOT!

He squirms in his seat and points at the CB radio.

"People are listening to us. Keep it down!"

Oh my God. This dude is nuts. I can't believe I stopped to pick up this guy. I roll my eyes and steer the cab to the curb.

"What's the deal?"

You have to go, buddy. I point to the street.

Sorry. Good luck.

He mournfully exits the cab.

As I'm driving away, I hear him yell, "I know you know where my wife's at!"

THE JAPANESE-MEXICAN

Pick up: a cheap motel on the North Side. I swing in. Room #122. Honk. Out comes a guy in his midforties. He's got spiky, gelled hair and a paisley shirt.

"I'm Mexican and Japanese. Born in Japan. Raised in Mexico."

His name is Jackie. He came to America for work and better wages.

"Trabajo!"

Our destination is a Western Union. It seems he is also broke.

"A friend wired me some money," he says, "and I want to go pick it up."

Not a good sign.

If the money's not there on the other side or it's late or it was never sent, I have to pay his fare. It's always something on the night shift.

We roll on. I explain to him that his situation is problematic and if he can't pay me, I will have to pay his fare and that isn't good. He thanks me for trusting him. Also, I think he is drunk.

"I really need a friend right now."

He wants to shake my hand. I shake his hand. Drunk people like to shake hands a lot. I tell him I have a five-handshake limit. After that, I cut you off. Jackie laughs. Slaps me on the shoulder and then he tries to shake my hand again. I do it.

"See? You don't have to be grumpy."

He reaches over and rubs my shoulder. I brush him off.

Hey now, little buddy. Stop that.

Now he's got me wondering if he is gay, which is fine. But I'm not gay. So, don't touch. I swat his hand away. He lets out a maniacal laugh and then tries to tickle me.

Hey, man. I'm driving!

He tries to tickle me again.

Look, you're going to have to stop that.

He laughs that crazy laugh again. Jackie is harmless, but definitely has boundary issues. I tell him that I am not gay.

"NO! I'm not gay either! I just like manly men!" He repeats this several times. "I'm not gay. I just like manly men!"

Just don't touch me while I'm driving, OK?

"I'm not gay either!"

No offense, I tell him, but you are acting very gay! He gets a kick out of that and once again laughs like a crazy man.

We arrive at the Western Union. He goes inside to fill out paperwork and retrieve the money sent to him. Ten minutes later, he walks out.

How'd it go? I ask.

"Fabulous!"

The transaction was successful, and he has his money. He flashes his new wad of cash. Good for him. And good for me. I don't have to pay his fare.

We roll out.

The new money in his pocket seems to fuel an extra level of craziness to his behavior.

He rolls down the window and screams into the night, "I have moneeeeeyyy!"

I tell him to settle down and put on his seatbelt.

He laughs and tries to tickle me again.

I warn him that if he attempts to tickle me again, I will kick him out of the cab. And like a true crazy man, he tries to do it again.

I pull the cab over to the side of the road and slam on the brakes.

Seriously, man. Get out of the cab, I say.

"OK. I'll stop."

Seriously, I'll kick you out. You have to stop doing that.

"But I like manly men!" He laughs.

I shake my head and roll on.

BUSINESS CLASS

This guy's a piece of work. Another graduate of the Ted Bundy School of Sociopaths. I'll refer to him as Bob.

Bob says he loves "pussy and money."

"Not in that order."

He's got a DUI.

"That's why I'm in the cab."

Daddy's got money.

"I'm rich as shit."

Mommy didn't love him.

"She was a cold bitch."

He used to sell cocaine.

"I made good money."

But now he rarely does it.

"Special occasions," he says.

It becomes apparent this guy is a rich fuck-up.

He points to an office building.

"I own that."

I marvel at the amount of money and potential pissed away on rich assholes. He's probably never had a real job in his life. It's not the money that bothers me, it's the attitude of entitlement that comes with it. I don't care who you think you are. Sooner or later, the playing field gets flattened and true souls have their day in the black sun. Bob and I roll toward his house. Him talking. Me listening.

We arrive at his house and a weird thing happens. He turns and looks me in the eyes and sincerely thanks me.

"Thanks for listening to me talk. I needed that."

Very strange.

It catches me off guard. For the first time since he got in the cab, I can see the human being in him. The obnoxious front has evaporated. He is a forty-one-year-old little boy who has been shit on and neglected and probably abused like the rest of us for things he doesn't understand.

He shakes my hand three times and says thank you and goodbye like he doesn't want me to leave, like he doesn't want to be alone in his big empty house by himself, where he's been alone for a long time.

He's alone like each of us,
    Sitting silently in the dark
    With all the days and years stacked on top of one another
    Like a house of cards, ready at any minute to topple over.

He pays the fare and leaves. I sit in his driveway for a minute. Reflecting.
It's so strange when just enough light
    Shines through the cracks
    In your own heart
    And allows you to see things
    For what they really are,
    If only for a few seconds.

THE SOCIOPATH

I pick up a big guy—maybe six-foot-four—at a McDonald's. He wants to go to the Mardi Gras parade. He's got a dark vibe, possibly sociopathic. You can feel it. Like a rope about to pop. He says he's an ex-military police-man and that he hates cops. He doesn't explain why.

"I hate everybody and everything."

He's divorced.

"She was a bitch."

And he was recently fired from his job.

"They were assholes."

He then goes into a long, creepy list of all the terrible things he's done to people.

Smashed faces.

Burnt houses.

Put people in the hospital.

Stolen credit cards.

"I don't give a fuck."

He's a keeper.

He's got that something special about him that makes you want to hide your daughters and lock all your doors.

I drop him off on a side street near the parade route, wondering if there is a God.

THE SINGING TRAIN WRECK

Call to pick up at Motel 6.
I pull up
And see a woman in a parking lot.
Her bags are on the ground.
She is a Hurricane Katrina evacuee.
She's just been kicked out of her hotel.
"Fuck FEMA!"
She also just broke up with her boyfriend.
"Fuck him, too!"
We roll toward another motel.
Tall can of beer in her hand.
"I'm a crazy black woman, so don't fuck with me."
She talks the whole way.
About everything.
The boyfriend, Hurricane Katrina, Xanax, her kid, etc.
Then out of nowhere,
She begins to sing
In a hauntingly beautiful voice,
Like Billie Holiday.
I drive and listen.
Just taking it in.

    Her voice is like a lot of things
    I hope to never understand.

A BOTTLE OF DEAD DREAMS

I pass a couple cops rousting a drunk. He was asleep in some bushes near a charity hospital. The guy is dirty and missing a shirt.

I drive by and stare.

What's that guy's story?

Why'd he pick that place to sleep?

When you're homeless, how do you go about picking a good spot to sleep?

Do you just drink your bottle of wine and then walk until your legs tangle and you fall in a bush?

I watch as they cart him away.

I wonder where he is from.

Where was he born?

What happened to him?

What happens to all of us?

At what point does your life jump the tracks and you wake up in a bush with a bottle of dead dreams and two cops standing over you?

TEX TEXARKANA

Pick up at a biker bar. I roll up. There's a gathering of big dudes with big motorcycles outside. I nod at them, bop the horn. The bikers stare and sip beer. No one moves. No one comes out. I kill the cab. Walk inside. It's loud. A lot of drunk folks. Jukebox blasting. I signal the bartender.

Who called a cab? I ask.

She points to an older guy in a cowboy hat.

I approach and call him Tex, because he looks like a "Tex."

Hey, Tex. Are you ready to roll?

"You bet I'm ready!"

I lead. Tex follows.

We climb in the cab. Where are we going?

Tex stares into the void and doesn't answer for a long time.

"You know what? I can't remember the name of my hotel."

That's a problem, I inform him.

We roll on anyway. He scans the hard drive of his brain.

"It was right up the road."

Does anything around here look familiar? I ask.

"No, not really."

How about I take you to any hotel? You can get some sleep and figure it out in the morning.

"Good enough!"

I drive him to the nearest hotel, a Days Inn. We pull up, and I walk him into the lobby. Tex scissor-steps his way up to the counter. I tell the hotel clerk that his nickname is Tex Texarkana. He's a famous cattle wrestler and he needs a room. Tex nods. We shake hands and I leave. Never to see him again.

The cab life moves fast. The whole episode, from the biker bar to the hotel, probably only took six minutes. This job is good for that. It trains and conditions you to deal with unusual situations, as if you're doing nothing more than rolling donuts at a bakery except in this case the donut is Tex and he's already baked.

SHILOH TRAILER PARK

Saturday night. I pick up a mother and her seventeen-year-old son from a bowling alley. She took him bowling tonight. Just the two of them, mother and son. Single mom trying to keep him out of trouble. Living in the ghetto. Things could go either way.

She gives me their address. It's Shiloh Trailer Park, located out in the country, north of Lafayette. It's a haunted and crumbling collection of over one hundred ragged, bombed-out trailers. The whole place is busted up, bent, discolored, ripped, rolled over, and broken down. I feel sorry for the poor folks that live there. It's filled with all stripes of rural crackheads, disadvantaged kids, deadbeats, wife-punchers, dog-beaters, pill-poppers, defeated persons, and good old working-class folks. When you roll through there, drifters dart between the trailers, commiserating with dogs and demons in shadow and in dirt.

Be glad you have no reason to go there.

The mother makes polite conversation. I return it in kind.

Nice lady.

I drop them off. She pays and tips me two dollars. I try to wave it off, but she insists. It may not seem like much, but when you are poor, two dollars is a lot to be giving away. I've had rich folks in the cab who wouldn't even tip one dollar on a fifty-dollar cab ride. Fuck them. I try to give her the money back, but she anticipates my move and quickly turns and walks away.

Then, she turns back around, smiles, and waves goodbye.

What a sweetheart.

Good people.

You got to love them,

Because there aren't enough of them around.

BODY ODOR LADY

A woman climbs in the cab.
She is going to the grocery store.
As we roll, I get a whiff of some bad body odor.
This poor woman smells bad.
I roll down all the windows and try to ignore it.
Pretend I need some fresh air.
Sad thing is,
This woman is really nice.
Friendly.
Maybe that's why no one
Has the heart to tell her
She smells bad.

SHOP TALK

2:54 a.m. The night slows to a crawl. The cabdrivers of the night shift gather at the Greyhound bus station, waiting for calls. We park side to side, talking shit. Slow nights are always like this. The conversation is hilarious at times. Who is fucking who? Which driver is fucking which dispatcher? Who's smoking crack in the cab? What driver wrecked which cab? Who got fired? Who is cutting calls? Who's about to get fired? Who is selling pills out of the cab?

The funniest conversation is when they start talking about the customers and various fucked-up calls they had to deal with. Since drivers often can't remember many of the names of customers, they refer to them by their addresses.

"Oh, don't ever pick up 3061 Madison. That woman is crazy."

"Not as bad as 7142 Duval. That motherfucker ran on me!"

"No, the worst is 2098 Pershing. He's got problems."

"Dude at the Chicken Shack, always complaining."

"Not as much as the dude that works at the power plant on Walker."

Numbers and streets, that's all you remember after a while. That and the destinations.

It's a blur of numbers
And faces
And endless streets
Dragging along behind you.

TOP TEN THINGS FOUND IN A CAB

Loose change
Combs
Chapstick
Lipstick and makeup
Candy
Lighters
Knives
Gum
Business cards
Cell phones

A CRACK IN THE SUN

4:24 p.m. The dispatcher gives me a call to pick up at a notorious drug spot off Madeline Street. It's an abandoned residence now serving as a crack house—a condemned shack, wood like wet Ouija boards, gashed windows, weeds everywhere. Nothing but completely insane crack addicts, rattling around like broken parts in a pinball machine.

I pull up.

Honk.

Out comes a white woman, midthirties, skinny as a baseball bat. I know she is going to cause me trouble. I can feel it. She came out of that house wiggling strangely, limbs flapping. This is a common idiosyncrasy of many crack addicts; they have a weird style of walking. I ready myself for some hassles.

Addiction is a horrible thing. I've been there myself. I know the personal horrors that go with full-on addiction, and sadly, crackheads seem to have it the worst. No junkie is trustworthy, but crackheads are even more sketchy. They've always got some insane drama attached to the things they do. No matter how simple the task, there is no straight line. They're desperate. They don't think straight and when they're super fucking high on crack, they're willing to do anything to get what they want. I think about pulling away and refusing the call, right there, but I stay and wait.

Two crackheads follow the woman out of the house. They attempt to convince her to stay. She ignores them. Climbs in the cab. Her name is Mary. She wants to go to a residence on the other side of town. Supposedly, her ex-husband left her some money on the back porch of his house. She wants to go get it. I stop the cab. This doesn't sound good. Crackhead. No money. Porch. Ex-husband. Going across town.

I ask for her ex-husband's phone number. She gives it to me. I call him. He answers and confirms her story. I take a deep breath and we roll. We plow into five o'clock traffic. Mary squiggles around in her seat and rolls down every window in the cab while talking drug-fueled gibberish. We roll past kids in buses, moms in minivans, and business folk headed home as she hangs her head out of the window like a dog on an afternoon joyride.

She shares bits of her story.

She's from New Orleans.

Her first husband was shot in the head during a drug deal.

108

"He died next to me."

We roll on.

At a red light, a family in a minivan idles next to us. They stare at her in horror. Mary in the afternoon. They don't know what to make of her. She's from a different planet. Mary sees a poodle in the car. She stares at it. She and the poodle lock eyes in a weird trance. The traffic light turns green. Mary starts to cry. The dog stares back.

Mary starts punching the dashboard.

"I once had a dog named Rufus!"

Finally, we reach our destination: the ex-husband's house.

Mary jumps out, runs around to the back of the house.

I wait.

She returns with an envelope.

We roll and she counts the money. One hundred dollars. She hands me twenty dollars, and I ask where she wants to go now.

Back to the crack house, of course.

We roll in that direction. Traffic is even worse now and she's even more geeked out and anxious than before. I'd really like to help her, to talk some sense to her. But she won't listen. There's nothing one can do. I can't save the world. I can't save her. I can barely save myself. All I can do is drive her across town without any major incidents.

Just as before, she hangs out the window, waves her arms around. She screams at unsuspecting common folk. I see a woman gasp as we pass her.

Crack arms flailing.

Hair in a spidery swirl.

We're a nightmare rolling through their world.

I grip the wheel, run a few yellow lights, take a few shortcuts through parking lots, speed down congested streets. People stare at us. Mary's madness has intensified my own. We're all varying degrees of crazy. I round the last corner, and there's the crack house.

The crackheads are waiting outside. Waiting for her.

Waiting in the dirt and dust.

Sun rats at the end of the world.

Shuffling zeros in the shade.

Mary grabs her stuff. She thanks me for the ride. I pull away and watch them slowly shuffle into the house to conduct whatever insane sorceries they have planned with that eighty dollars.

CHESTER

I get a call to pick up a guy going to work at Walmart. Just on some idiotic whim, as he jumps in the cab I say, "How are you doing, Chester?"

He looks at me strangely.

"How'd you know my last name?" he says.

I didn't, I say.

"My name's Jon Chester."

He pulls out his wallet and shows me his ID.

And there it is: Jon Chester.

CINDERELLA

Cinderella is a hooker. She's a regular in the cabs. She's been on the street for three years. Interesting fact: she's a former schoolteacher from Iberia Parish. Now she's hooked on crack. It could happen to anyone. She's been up for a week.

"How do I look since you saw me last?"

Worse, I say.

"Thanks a lot."

Where to?

"St. Francis Motel."

St. Francis Motel is the lowest of the low-rent motels in town.

What are you going to do over there? I ask.

"I'm going to fuck some Mexicans."

Oh.

"It won't take long. They fuck fast and come quick."

How long would you guess?

"Sixty seconds."

I drop her off at the motel room. A door opens. Several Mexican laborers appear. She walks in. It's not a fairy tale. It's just a nightmare, and it's everywhere that drugs are.

CUP OF PISS

Pick up at a Duson trailer park. I roll up. Honk. Out comes a wiry dude, midforties. He hops in the front seat.

Where are we going?

"Are you cool?"

Sigh.

That question means only one thing: he is looking for drugs. I tell him I'll take him wherever he wants to go as long as he conducts himself in a "professional" manner and doesn't do anything stupid. It's his business. I don't care. All I care about is getting in and out safely with minimal hassle. I explain that if we're going into a ghetto neighborhood to score drugs, there is an unofficial ten- to twenty-dollar "surcharge" on top of the price of the fare. For this amount, I'll watch his back and keep shit cool. That's the deal. Period. Are you cool with that?

"I guess."

Well, you better be sure before we drive into whatever shithole you want to cop drugs.

He pisses and moans, gripes about the surcharge.

Do you want to go or not? That's the deal.

"OK. Let's go!"

Already, I don't like this guy. He's got a bad vibe.

We roll to his drug spot on the west side of town. It's some low-rent apartments where street dealers hustle crack on a dark corner. We locate the spot. I remind him to handle his business, no bullshit. If you get beat, you get beat. That's part of the game. Copping drugs on the street is a wacky science. You never know what you're going to get and who you'll be dealing with.

"I know what I'm doing."

Yeah, right.

We pull in, and a dealer approaches his window. They talk. He haggles with the dealer. Then, the dealer hands him a few rocks. The passenger begins inspecting the rocks before handing over the money. Bad move. He's taking too long. Things begin to get tense. Come on, you asshole.

Give him the money! I say.

I inch the cab forward. He finally gives him the money.

We roll out.

On the way back to his home, he clenches the crack in his fist. He's quiet and anticipating the high. We pull up to his trailer. The fare is forty-five dollars, including the surcharge.

"I have to get the rest of the money inside."

OK.

He goes inside to grab the money.

I have to piss. It's below freezing outside, so I grab my Big Gulp cup, empty the ice out, and take a long, slow piss into the cup. As I'm finishing up, the guy comes out. I put the cup back in the dashboard cup holder. Half full. He hops in the front seat.

What you got?

He hands me a wad of crumpled bills. I count it. It's only thirty-two dollars total.

I tell him that's not good enough. It doesn't even cover the basic fare *without* the surcharge. He bitches and gripes, cursing. You weasel. I shake my head. That's not the deal we had. Come on, motherfucker.

The guy squirms in the seat. He swings his arm toward me and attempts to stab me with an ink pen.

I block his arm.

We tussle in the cab.

I slap him in the head.

In the chaos, one of us bumps the cup of piss and it almost spills over.

I catch the cup and toss it in his face.

I can't help but laugh.

Dude hops out of the cab.

Cussing.

"Why'd you do that?!" he asks.

Because you're an asshole, that's why.

I shake my head.

This guy is hopeless.

I roll out. Disgusted with him.

What a creep.

At least he was good for a laugh.

THE CELL PHONE THIEVES

Pick up: a house. My passengers are a thug and his girlfriend. They're going to a house near Edison Park. Same block where some dude got shot and killed the other night. Six-dollar call. I'll call this guy Jeezy. Like everyone, he complains about the price of the fare.

"Six dollars? Why so much?"

I sigh. It's just the way it is, dude.

They climb in and we roll. It's a short trip. But a weird thing happens on the ride: my cell phone rings from the back seat. I feel around. I can't find it. It's not in any of my pockets. It's not crammed in the seat. The dispatcher calls over the CB and gives me another call. I get distracted for a minute, logging the call in my notebook.

We arrive at Jeezy's house on Edison Street. He pays the fare and gives me some foul attitude. I'm not sure why, sometimes people are just assholes. They exit and walk off.

I immediately jump out and searched the back of the cab for my cell phone. I still can't find it. Anywhere. This is not good. All my contacts are on that phone. I radio the dispatcher and ask him to call my cell in the hopes of locating it in the cab. I wait and search. No ring. No phone. No nothing. Fuck.

While I am searching the cab for my phone. Jeezy walks up behind me. I'm still parked in front of his house.

"What are you still doing here?" he asks.

I'm looking for my cell phone, dude.

"Oh."

Did you or your girlfriend happen to see it in the back seat?

"Fuck no, nigga! I ain't got your motherfucking cell phone!"

I stare blankly at him. Try to stay calm, I tell myself.

"You gotta get your ass out of here. You can't be sitting out here in front of my house, looking for your damn cell phone."

I'm seeing red flags all over the motherfucking place now. Mostly because this dude is a little adamant about me "getting my ass out of here."

I'm not moving the cab until I find it, I inform him.

I turn my back on him and continue searching the cab. Turning my back on him is a symbolic gesture. It says: You are not a threat to me, and I have no fear of anything you do. I'm talking shit, though—I am kind of scared of what kind of kooky shit could happen. But I need my phone back.

"Man, get your ass outta here with your old lost-ass cell phone!"

Jeezy walks back to the house.

To his back I repeat: I ain't going nowhere till I get it back.

I continue the search and find nothing. This is not a great situation. I'm in a fucked-up neighborhood where somebody got shot recently, and this whole episode could easily escalate into something bad.

Pause.

How do I get myself into this shit? Should I cut my losses? Drive away and continue the night's shift? Play it safe? I'm almost 99 percent positive this Jeezy clown has my phone. I came to work with it, so I know I didn't lose it earlier. My guess is that my phone slid out of my pocket and fell onto the floor in the back seat where they picked it up and pocketed it after hearing it ring. It's simple. That's got to be it. Getting it back will NOT be simple. Conclusion: No fucking way am I leaving here without my cell phone. It's decided.

I take a deep breath. I walk up to the house and knock on the door. The door opens quickly as if they were waiting for me. A black man in his late-fifties jerks open the door. I'm guessing he is Jeezy's father. We'll call him Too Tall.

Too Tall immediately gets in my face.

"Look, man! Ain't nobody got your damn cell phone! Now, get away from my house! We done told you we ain't got it!"

Jeezy is probably hiding in the back room.

I try to stay calm and relaxed. All I want is my phone back, I tell him. I don't care who took it or why. I just want it back. That is my phone and I'm not leaving without it.

My short speech has no effect on Too Tall. I even offer to pay them twenty dollars if they will just give it back to me. No questions asked. No response.

I go back to the cab, which is still parked in the street in front of their house. A few minutes later, Too Tall and Jeezy appear in their front yard.

"You need to get your ass out of here and off my property!"

Sigh. What a couple of assholes. They definitely have my phone.

I tell them again that I am not leaving until I get my cell phone. I am on public property. I can stay here as long as I want.

I've made up my mind. I lose my grip on staying relaxed and calm and lay into them with a dose of vitriol.

I may be a white boy in the ghetto about to get jumped, but I ain't leaving until I get my phone back. You can yell all you want. I don't care anymore. Fuck you. Fuck your lies. Fuck your ghetto. Fuck this cab. Fuck my job and fuck everything else I have no control over. Fuck it all. I just want my phone. And I ain't leaving.

They don't like that speech either.

"I'm calling the police," says Too Tall.

You know what? I say. I'll do the same. Let's both call them.

Too Tall and Jeezy stand in the yard, not moving, watching me. I climb in the cab, grab the CB, and radio the dispatcher to call all the police.

"What you got, Driver Four?"

10-6, I reply.

"You sure you want to 10-6?" he asks.

10-4. The customer stole my phone. I'm not leaving till I get it back.

"Stand by. I'm calling them now," says the dispatcher.

Too Tall and Jeezy stand in their yard and watch me.

I just notified my dispatcher to call the police, I inform them.

"Man, fuck your dispatcher!"

They turn to go back in the house.

This will be interesting. I sit in the cab and wait. Five, ten, fifteen minutes pass. The police have yet to show up. I guess they've got more important stuff to do. I sit in the cab and keep watch on the house. Twenty minutes after radioing the police code, Jeezy reappears in the yard.

He yells at me.

"Get your ass outta here, man! You are going to get hurt. We don't play that bullshit! Ain't nobody got your damn phone!"

I stare at him unblinking. Silent.

Jeezy goes back to the house. Another ten minutes pass, still no cops. It's been thirty minutes since I made the police call. Now Too Tall appears. He hollers at me from the yard. Same routine.

"You need to get the fuck on out of here!"

I stare at him poker faced. Same as Jeezy. Silent.

I don't know what I'm doing, but I'm doing it. For better or worse.

Every few minutes, either Too Tall or Jeezy exit the house and attempt to scare me off with more warnings and threats. Fuck them. All I want is my phone back. They go back to the house. Then things get quiet. No cops. No Too Tall. No Jeezy. Guess they got tired of trying to scare me off.

I sit and wait for the cops. It's now been forty-five minutes since I made the call to dispatch. Still no cops. Fuck the police, too. Nobody gives a fuck about you unless you've got money or power or property. I'm just an out-of-work musician, writer, and cabdriver trying to get my phone back. I sit and wait.

Now, it's one hour since the police call. I'm starting to lose faith in the endeavor. Then, once again, Jeezy appears in the yard. He looks around, up and down the street, and then approaches the cab very slowly.

I'm not sure what he's doing this time. I wonder if he's got a gun. I watch him closely. He cautiously gazes around and approaches the cab. We lock eyes. He stares at me. I stare at him.

What's up? I ask.

Silence.

He slowly reaches into his pocket. I tense up.

He pulls my phone from his pocket and tosses it at me through the open window.

"Where's my twenty dollars?" he asks.

Yes! My phone.

Man, FUCK YOUR twenty dollars! I yell.

I drop the cab into DRIVE and roll the hell out of there. I'm triumphant, ecstatic, and overjoyed. I stood up to those jerks and got my damn cell phone back.

Take that!

Life lesson: when everything is against you, and things don't look good, but you know you're right, GO ALL IN AND GET THAT MOTHEFUCKING PHONE BACK!

See you later, assholes.

RANDIMONIUM

One of the other night shift drivers had a crazy fare last night. It's a good story.

The cabdriver's name is Randy. He's a longhaired Hispanic guy from California now living in Louisiana. During a lull in the shift, Randy picks up a guy named Butch. Butch owns a construction company, has a lot of money. Butch wants to party all night and wants to find a prostitute.

Can Randy help him out? YES.

Randy drives Butch to the hot spots where streetwalkers congregate. He locates two women. Butch hires them both. They climb in the cab and Randy drives them all back to Butch's hotel room, where the party starts. Randy gets paid and leaves.

Butch calls Randy a few hours later.

"Come pick me up. I need to make a beer run," he asks.

Randy returns to the hotel and picks up Butch. The prostitutes stay in the room. Randy and Butch go to a store, buy beer. When they return to the hotel, Butch asks Randy to stop by the hotel office to get an extra key. Randy does it.

As Butch exits the office, he stops.

He looks across the parking lot, sees something. Butch runs and jumps in the cab, screaming, "Go, Go, Go!"

Randy punches the accelerator just as a big 4x4 truck speeds toward them and narrowly misses hitting the cab.

"Who is that?" Randy screams.

"My wife!" says Butch.

"Oh, shit!" says Randy.

Randy guns the motor on the cab. He and Butch race out of the parking and into the streets. The wife follows them.

Thus begins a ten-minute car chase. They haul ass up and down the back streets and through an industrial park near the hotel, reaching high speeds. The wife stays with them. Her truck, which is actually Butch's truck, has been modified.

"It's got extra horsepower," says Butch.

Randy tries to lose her, but he can't shake her. That modified truck stays right on their asses, growling up and down the streets like a raging monster, muffler rattling.

Randy makes a bad decision. In the blur of the chase, he turns down a dead-end street and gets cornered by the wife in the monster truck. Before Randy can stop and reverse direction, the wife plows straight into the rear of the cab.

BOOM!

Unsatisfied with the damage, the wife hits them again. And again. Numerous times. She guns the monster truck and begins pushing the cab off the road and into a ditch.

Sensing no other alternative—and his defeat—Butch climbs out of the cab and tries to reason with his wife. They argue and scream in the night. But not much is accomplished in their exchange. The wife speeds away in the monster truck.

Randy calls the police and the cabstand, alerting them to the recent events. Police arrive on the scene. The cab is towed back to the yard. Butch and Randy spend the next hour filing police reports and attempting to explain what the fuck just happened.

End of story.

EMERGENCY ROOM

Call to pick up near Cameron Street. I pull up to the given address. Honk.
Lights out.

No one home.

I wait.

Finally, I see a man walk out of the shadows. It's Henry, a local homeless
guy. I've seen him before, usually sleeping on benches in the downtown area.
Henry slowly walks toward the cab. He climbs into the front seat. Under the
harsh illumination of the interior bulb of the cab, I see that Henry's head and
face are covered in blood and cuts. Both eyes are swollen like a boxer. There
is blood splatter on his shirt.

What happened to you?

"I got jumped by three teenagers outside a bar."

Are you serious?

"I ran away and hid behind this house. The people next door saw me and
called a cab."

Why didn't they call a cop? Or an ambulance?

"I guess they didn't want the hassle."

I roll my eyes.

"They just want it to go away."

I steer the cab toward the charity hospital.

"I don't have any money," he says. "They took that, too."

I tell him not to worry about it.

Jesus Christ. What is wrong with people?

We roll out.

Henry is dazed and moaning.

"I'm cold."

I wonder if he's going into shock.

I speed over to the hospital. We pull up to the emergency room. I run in
and locate a nurse. A security guard is standing next to her.

Can we get some help? I have a man in my cab who is hurt.

They don't move an inch. They just stare at me. I guess if you don't arrive
in an ambulance, you are expected to walk in on your own two feet. I return
to the cab and help Henry get out. I walk him inside the hospital. A nurse
takes him from there.

As I leave, he turns, and we make eye contact.
His eyes are sad and scared.
And so are mine.

LOUISIANA SERIAL KILLER

I pick up an older black couple. They're going to eat dinner at a nice restaurant. Sweet folks. Married for over twenty-five years. They laugh and sit close in the back seat. So cute. I love seeing older couples that have stayed together.

"We haven't taken a cab in years," they say.

We make small talk. They're Hurricane Katrina evacuees from New Orleans. They lost their house in the flood, lost everything.

"But that was nothing in comparison to losing my daughter," the man says.

I ask what he means by that.

He goes into a long, detailed explanation of how his daughter was one of the victims of Louisiana serial killer Derrick Todd Lee, who was found responsible for the deaths of seven women in the Baton Rouge and Lafayette areas. Their daughter was an LSU graduate student.

What do you say to something like that? It's heartbreaking.

In a calm and emotionally measured manner, he explains the details of her death and the specifics of the case.

After he is done speaking, the cab falls silent
And we are engulfed with the rush of the wind
Blowing through the open windows.

TECHNICAL KNOCKOUT

It's a slow night. While parked downtown, a black guy in his midthirties walks up and politely asks me for a ride. His name is Terrell. His destination is not far, so I decide to take the ride.

Terrell jumps in the front seat.

We roll.

Immediately after picking up Terrell, the dispatcher calls and tells me to pick up two guys around the corner at a downtown bar. Fuck it. I'll knock out both calls together. We turn the corner and I locate the two men: two white guys in their midforties.

I pull up.

They get into the seat back. It's obvious they are very drunk.

Where to?

"Comfort Inn."

I'll refer to these guys as Manny and Moe. They make friendly chatter. For no apparent reason, Manny, in a drunken haze, decides to reach up behind Terrell (in the front seat), and put him in a headlock/chokehold.

Unbelievable. Drunk people do some stupid shit.

Instantly, I slam on the brakes and yell loudly at Manny.

LET HIM GO RIGHT NOW!

Through the stranglehold of Manny's arms, I can see Terrell's big, round, panicked eyes. He looks terrified.

Let him go! I scream.

Manny releases him. Terrell frantically fumbles with the door handle, exits the cab and runs off. Gone.

What the fuck is your problem?! I ask Manny.

"I was just messing with him," says Manny. Unbelievable.

I warn Manny that if he tries anything like that again, I will kick him out of the cab. I reach over and pull Terrell's door shut, which was left open upon his quick exit.

We roll. The cab is silent. I navigate through the downtown streets.

And then . . .

I feel Manny's arms around my neck.

What the fuck?

Now he is putting me in a headlock/chokehold.

Un-fucking-believable.

I slam the breaks and bring the cab to a stop.

In one fluid movement, I do three things:

    1. Throw the gear shift into PARK.

    2. Kick open my door.

    3. Quickly untangle and slide myself out from his chokehold.

With that completed, I hop out of the cab and look around. Now what am I going to do? These assholes are still sitting in the back seat of my cab.

I lean into the cab, cock my fist back, and punch in the general direction of where Manny's face is. It lands! It's a good punch. I just aimed in his general direction and let it fly. I don't think I've ever punched anyone so perfectly in my life. Manny's nose explodes like a blood bag. Blood squirts everywhere.

I pause and look at him. His glasses are mashed up and crooked on his face. He's dazed and doesn't seem to realize what just happened to him. Good.

Get the fuck out of the cab! I yell.

He steps out. His busted nose is bleeding down his shirt. I climb back in the cab, throw it in gear, and roll out. Then I realize his friend is still in the back seat. He apologizes for Manny.

"I barely know the guy," he says. "We're in town for work."

You should've known he was an idiot. I drop Moe off at his hotel. Then I pause.

I sit in the parking lot and catch my breath. I happen to glance down at my notebook. It's open to my log sheet of the night's calls. It's covered with Manny's blood.

Gross.

Chapter 3
THE GRIND

ONLY THE DUST

Today marks my third year driving a cab. The chaos is now routine.
I've become acclimated
    To the violence
    The prostitutes
    The addicts
    The crazies
    The drunks
    The twelve-hour night shifts.
It is all normal now.
It's been a strange experience,
    Sprinting through the dark marsh of the Deep South
    Night after night.
The streets go on forever.
One day it will all be dust.
When the mountains crumble,
    I will nod at the inevitability of the dust.
One day
This will all be gone.
    No televisions
    No cell phones
    No money
    No people.
Just the quiet earth.
The sun will rise beautifully
From the horizon
But only the dust
Will be there
To receive it.

HEART CALIBRATION

Pick up at the old people projects. My passenger is a sweet old black man going to the charity hospital. His bag is packed. He appears nervous.

How are you doing?

"I'm not feeling too good right now," he says.

What's wrong?

"My blood pressure is riding high. I'm dizzy. I want to make sure I ain't dying."

OK. How come your wife isn't coming with you?

"She's gone; it's just me now. Everybody done died off."

I feel my heart twist in my chest, sweet old man.

We talk and roll through the night, eventually arriving at the hospital. I help him out of the cab. He thanks me.

I watch him walk in. His shirt is tucked into his jeans. He's got an industrious little shuffle to his walk. A few little tears squeeze out of my eyes as I watch him walk away.

Sometimes when you're too wound up and consumed with your own bullshit, it's nice to have an experience that recalibrates your heart. It reminds you that you are human. It's as if for a few brief minutes, God lets you peek inside someone else's soul.

You are never ready for it.

It just happens.

And it sets you straight for a while.

You forget all your own problems.

They don't seem as big or stressful.

And you feel a strange kinship with your fellow humans,

Because you realize they are fragile

And possibly broken just like you.

THE GAMBLER

Fifty-four years old.
He is a gambler.
Full-time.
He plays poker in backrooms.
"That's my only job."
Interesting.
"I was also a sniper in the Marines."
How many people have you killed?
"Eight."
What is the most money you've ever won in a poker game?
"$17,000."
Lost?
"$1,800."
Have you ever seen someone pull a gun in a card game?
He pulls up his shirt and shows me a scar on his stomach.
"Yes."

PISSING ON THE STARS

Pick up at a bar. It's another drunkard. Middle-aged. Wasted. Bar hopping. He wants to go to another bar. We roll. Halfway there, he changes his mind and wants to go to a different bar. I swing the cab in that direction. Five minutes later, he changes his mind again and wants to go to a third bar that he just remembered.

I shake my head and pull the cab into a dark, deserted empty lot.

"What are you doing?" he asks.

I have to piss.

All this turning around is making it more urgent. I suggest that while I'm pissing, he can make up his mind as to where he wants to go. He stares at me strangely.

OK?

"Whatever." He sits quietly in the cab.

Then I hear him sobbing.

What's wrong, brother?

He sits and fidgets with his empty bottle of beer. He starts to talk about his brother.

"He died in a car accident."

His family.

"They're all fucked up."

His ex-girlfriend.

"She's crazy."

His job.

"It sucks."

I nod quietly and tell him it'll be OK. Let it go.

He nods back at me, shakes my hand. I step out to piss. He stays in the cab. Nobody around. I piss beneath the stars, staring up at them, spacing out.

Then, out of nowhere, a police car races into the vacant lot we are parked in and speeds toward us, lights flashing, siren chirping. What the fuck is going on now?! I say to myself.

A cop hops out.

"What are you doing here?" he asks.

I'm on the clock and taking a piss. Don't you see the cab?

"We got a report of some drug activity back here."

I shake my head.

No, I'm just doing my job.

Silence.

Then, "I'm going to need to see your ID and registration for the cab."

Roll my eyes. I hand him the paperwork.

He walks back to his cop car and runs my ID and the license plates.

What a douchebag. I stand there, waiting.

Cop returns. Hands me my driver's license.

"Well, it seems a little weird. But I guess I can let it go," he says.

Why wouldn't you? We're not doing anything.

"Have a good night," he says. The cop rolls off. I stare up at the stars and step into the cab. I look over at my passenger. He's passed out. Asleep. Head against the seat belt. Mouth open, drooling a bit.

I start the cab and sigh.

What the fuck am I doing with my life?

EXODUS

Call to pick up at a halfway house. As I roll up, there is a man standing in front with a bag and a small TV in a box. He hops in.

What's with the TV?

"I just got kicked out of the halfway house."

Why?

"Failed a drug test."

He relapsed last night.

"I slipped up. Smoked a rock."

Now he's out on the streets. He's bummed. Lost.

Where to?

He wants to go to an appliance store.

"I'm going to return the TV and use the money to buy a bus ticket to a detox center in Baton Rouge."

Good plan.

We roll and talk.

"I wrecked six cars in eight years." Multiple DUIs. Jail time. Ruined relationships.

We pull up to the store. He goes in. I wait. He returns ten minutes later with money in his hand. He seems like a good dude. I offer not to charge him for the cab ride. I point the cab toward the Greyhound station, but now he wants to make a stop on the way.

Where at?

He names some cross streets in the ghetto. Red flag. It's a dope spot in the hood.

I shake my head.

You sure that's where you want to go?

"Yep."

It is your life.

I drop him off at the dope spot. He disappears into the jungle of the streets.

This is definitely not rehab.

THE WHIRLYBIRD

Call to pick up at the mental health facility. Out walks a woman in her midforties.

We roll.

Where to?

"The Greyhound station."

How are you doing tonight?

"My husband left me."

Where did he go?

"He left with the carnival. We're both carnival workers."

Why did he leave you?

"He fell in love with the ring-toss girl."

How did you end up in the mental hospital?

"I got drunk and went crazy."

How crazy?

"I hit him in the head with a ball-peen hammer. He hit the ground. They called the cops. And I ran off and hid behind the Whirlybird. It's a carnival ride."

Yes, it sure as hell is.

MEASURED DOSES

I pick up an older guy in the downtown area. He's going to the bowling alley. He is loud and talks a lot, making comments on everything we pass on the drive.

"You see that overpass?"

Yes.

"It took them two years to make that. I worked concrete for twenty-two years. Hard work. Nobody wants to pour concrete. That's hard work! Your skinny ass couldn't pour no concrete. I bet you ain't never poured concrete in your life. You kids don't know what hard work is. My ex-wife never worked a damn day in her life! I got forty years of retirement coming my way. You drive bad, boy! You kids don't know how to drive! I lived in Chicago. 1972. Met a lot of fine women out there. I know how to treat a woman! A woman needs to be treated right. That is, if you want to keep them! You keep them on a short leash, or they'll try to get over on you. See that traffic light? I installed traffic lights for three years in Atlanta. Did it till I seen a man hang himself. He rigged up wrong to the power line. Electrified himself. Shocked his body straight as a board! Left him hanging upside down, traffic passing by beneath him. Took the fire truck fifteen minutes to get there. He was dead when they pulled up! I quit that day. Oh, no! You ain't going to fry me like that I told them! William Jefferson Bennett ain't going out like that! Hell no! Not me, partner!"

Some people come in measured doses.

Others do not.

TABLE FOR ONE

I pick up a young, black guy in his late twenties. He is going to a restaurant to eat, alone. He tells me he's a janitor. He loves his job. Feels lucky to have it.

"It's better than my last job."

He was a garbage man.

"That was hard," he says.

Now he is a janitor, and he doesn't have to break his back. He is thankful for that. He makes about two hundred dollars a week. He can live on that amount. When he has a little extra money, he gets dressed up and he treats himself to a meal at a restaurant. Like tonight. He eats alone because he is single. He enjoys it as best he can.

Once in a while, amidst the teeming grind of humanity, filled with nameless faces, faceless names, petty assholes, misguided idiots, fools and bastards of all stripe, with everyone trying to get one over on you and hustle you for some kind of bullshit, real or imagined, suddenly the sea parts and you get a momentary glimpse at the soul of another human being with no malice or meanness in their heart.

It's like someone flicked on a light switch in a forgotten corner of your heart. And it shocks your system back into alignment with the light. You close your eyes and nod in awe and in humility.

Because secretly you know

This is how you should feel all the time.

HOUSEWIFE IN THE GHETTO

It's late in the shift. I get a call to pick up in an upper-middle-class suburb. Roll up. Honk. Out comes a housewife, midforties, Caucasian. She is wearing a cotton-pullover dress with white sneakers.

She tells me her name is Maggie.

"Are you the cabdriver?"

I look around. I think so. Where to?

She gives me an address located deep in the ghetto. We roll. She doesn't look like a drug addict and does not mention drugs, so I'm not sure what to think about her. As we near her destination, she points to a convenience store.

We stop. She goes in. Curious, I watch. First guy she sees, she grabs him by the arm and takes him to the side. They talk. They both walk out and get in the cab. He gives me directions to an address a few blocks up the road. It is on a dead-end street bordered by a drainage canal.

We arrive.

"I'll be right back," she says.

OK.

They both exit the cab.

It's 2:51 a.m. The streets are empty. I watch them cross an empty lot, walk along the canal, and proceed down a trail that leads to a nearby housing project. I wait.

After ten minutes, I see no sign of either of them. I kill the ignition on the cab and lock it up. I walk across the lot and make my way down the trail to see if I can find them or make sense of this. I haven't been paid yet, so maybe they ran. I'm not sure what is going on.

I peek over a fence near the canal.

Nobody there.

I walk down the trail.

No one there.

I see nothing.

I pause.

Finally, I hear someone coming up the trail. I peak around. There she is, walking up the path. She's angry. I walk with her back to the cab.

How'd it go?

"I just got ripped off."

Well, it's not the best time of night nor the best location for that kind of thing.

"I know."

We walk back to the cab.

I drive her back to her suburban home.

At least she still has a chance to turn it all around.

DEAD IN A TREE

I pick up a middle-aged lady.
She explains that she suffered a head injury in a car accident years ago.
"That's why I talk a little slow."
She and her uncle were leaving a party.
They were having a good time.
It was a daytime party.
A family reunion.
He was drunk.
He was driving.
They were in his truck.
He lost control of the truck.
The truck went through a fence
    jumped a ditch
        hit an embankment
            and flipped upside down.
Her head went through the windshield.
When she awoke, she saw her uncle.
He was hanging in the branches of a tree.
Tangled.
He was dead.
He'd been thrown from the vehicle.
They were leaving a party.

NEVER GET OFF THE BUS

The dispatcher gives me a call to pick up at a local bail bonds place. It's located across the street from the jail. I pull up. Honk. Out comes a middle-aged white male. He looks like he hasn't slept in a week. He tells me his name is Rudy.

"I just got out of jail."

I figured that.

"I'm not having a great day."

What's the story?

Rudy was on a Greyhound bus going home to South Carolina. The bus stopped in Lafayette. Rudy was tired of being on the bus, so he decided to get off.

"I thought I'd hang out in Lafayette for a couple hours and catch a connecting bus later."

Rudy was looking for a good time.

"I like to party."

So, what happened?

At the bus station, Rudy met a guy. The guy was a scumbag, but Rudy didn't know it at the time. The Scumbag informed Rudy that he could get him a hotel room, some drugs, and a prostitute. Rudy liked this plan.

Scumbag and Rudy went to a motel. Scumbag paid for the room with a credit card and asked Rudy to reimburse him with cash, which Rudy did. True to his word, Scumbag got Rudy some crack and a prostitute.

"We partied all night. It was great."

However, at some point, the Scumbag disappeared. The next morning, Rudy was awakened to the sound of someone beating on his hotel room. He opened the door. It was the Lafayette Police Department. They charged him with credit card fraud. I guess Scumbag paid for the room with a stolen credit card. And they put it on Rudy. Then, the cops took Rudy to jail.

What's the moral to the story?

"Never get off the bus."

MAGNOLIA

Pick up.
Middle-aged guy,
Going to a wedding reception.
His license is suspended,
So he has to take the cab.
He's drunk
And carrying a magnolia flower.
He sits in the front
And lays the flower on the dash.
Why did you bring the flower?
"Because most cabs stink."

FIRE IN MY PANTS

Midway through the shift, I hit a bump in the road while lighting my cigarette. The cigarette bounces out of my mouth and down onto the floorboard of the cab somewhere. I reach around and try to find it as I drive. But I can't find it anywhere. I light another cigarette and forget about it.

Not long after that, the dispatcher gives me a call. I write down the address in the logbook and roll.

I arrive at the destination. Honk. Two girls get in. They are going across town. We roll.

"It smells like something is burning," one of them says.

I raise an eyebrow. Yeah?

"Yes, it smells like smoke."

I look around the interior of the cab. Now I smell it too. I feel around the floor of the cab again.

Pause.

I see smoke coming from my feet.

I notice that the cuff of my pants is burning.

I pull the cab to the curb.

Jump out.

The lit cigarette falls from the cuff of my pants.

One leg of my pants is on fire. I see threads burning.

I swat the fire out.

Toss away the cigarette.

The passengers laugh.

I climb back in the cab.

We roll on.

NOTES FROM THE BOSS

I arrive to work early for my shift. There are no cabs available at the moment, so I drink coffee in the break room and wait to get assigned a cab for my shift. Nearby there is a bulletin board where driver-related information is posted—usually it contains changes in company policy, rates, or local traffic laws. I notice two hand-written notices on the board that weren't there yesterday. I move closer to read them. They are both signed by Joe, the boss.

Sign #1

ATTENTION DRIVERS

ANY DRIVER CAUGHT STEALING ANOTHER DRIVER'S CALL
WILL BE FIRED!
ALSO, THE CAB IS NOT FOR FOOLING AROUND!
RIDE YOUR GIRLFRIEND AROUND
ON YOUR OWN GAS.
NOT ON MINE!

Sign #2

ATTENTION DRIVERS

NO DRIVERS ARE ALLOWED IN THE DISPATCH OFFICE!
DISPATCHERS ARE BUSY PEOPLE.
DO NOT MAKE ME KICK YOU OUT
AND EMBRACE [sic] YOU!

THE GAY COWBOY

2:04 a.m.

Call to pick up at a local gay bar. I pull up outside. Honk. The door to the club swings open. Out comes a man in a cowboy hat, late forties. He's stumbling drunk. He hops into the front seat and gives me his address.

We roll and make small talk. He is an interesting guy. He rolls down his window. I ask if it is too hot in the cab. He shakes his head.

"No, I've got to puke."

Roger that.

I quickly pull the cab to the curb. Before we can stop, Gay Cowboy does one of those "puke hiccups" where the first volley of puke comes thrusting from his mouth. A smattering of vomit lands on his cowboy shirt. He hangs his head out of the window.

We stop. He hops out of the cab and pukes in a ditch with his cowboy hat on. It is pure liquid. Whiskey and whatever. It flows like a stream.

He finishes and closes the door. We roll.

His shirt is a mess. He lights up a cigarette and talks about how much he drank.

"Too much in one day."

He started drinking at 10 a.m. and didn't stop until he left the gay bar.

"Not sure what got in me."

We arrive at his house: a little place out in the country. He pays me. No tip. I ask if he has some paper towels in his house that I can use to clean the puke splatter in the cab. He shakes his head.

"It's out of my hands," he says. "I've got to go lay down."

Old gay cowboy.

He doesn't give a shit.

Maybe that's why he's going home alone.

QUEEN BOOBS

Bar call. Downtown.

I roll up. Four drunken women tumble out. They're dressed up, bare feet with high-heeled shoes in their hands. Wasted. It is a busy time of night, so I have to put the rush on—meaning I've got about six other calls to field after this one. Getting drunk people to do things in a timely manner is not easy.

The girls pile in slowly. But one girl in particular is having problems. She is being cranky and difficult. She is also wearing a low-cut dress, out of which spill her enormous boobs. In addition to this, she's wearing a tiara and Mardi Gras beads. I refer to her as "Queen Boobs."

We are waiting on Queen Boobs to get in the cab. All of her friends are already seated in the cab. They yell at her to hurry up and get in. This triggers Queen Boobs, who apparently doesn't like to be rushed. A dark screw turns in her brain and she begins having a mildly psychotic episode in the street, cursing and screaming.

"FUCK OFF!"

I sense we are now entering dangerous Crazy Woman Territory.

Abruptly, she turns and walks off. I tell her to get in the cab.

"I would never get in the cab with you!"

I shake my head. She is like some wild lion. Her friends try to coax her into the cab, but she isn't having it. Instead, she walks off down the street with her heels in her hand and her boobs in the air.

"Leave her," one of her friends says. "She'll be fine."

I raise an eyebrow. Are you sure she'll be OK?

"She's probably going back to the bar."

Roger that.

I put the cab in gear, and we proceed to their destination. I drop the girls off. As an afterthought and against my better judgement, I backtrack and swing through downtown to look for Queen Boobs. If I can find her, I'll give her a ride. I'm not sure I could talk her into the cab, but it's worth a try.

After a couple laps around the area where I picked them up, I can't find her. There's no trace of her. I roll out.

Some women are tough like that.

They can handle themselves.

You can leave them anywhere and they will somehow make it home.

It could be through brute force of will or just dumb luck.

Not sure which.

But my guess is Queen Boobs has both on her side.

DETOX

Charlie is from Baytown, Texas.
He's a country guy.
Midfifties.
Ran with a biker gang.
He's got a rebel flag tattooed on his arm.
"I used to shoot a lot of cocaine," he says.
What made you quit?
"Prison."

DANIEL FLAHERTY

Pick up at a downtown bar. Roll up. Honk. Wait. Honk again.

A well-dressed guy appears. He waves at me. This must be him. He gets in. He is drunk. Very drunk. Where to?

"The Hilton."

He proudly tells me his name is Daniel Flaherty.

"I make a lot of money and I like to fuck women."

Of course you do, buddy.

"And I've got a boat."

He asks my name.

Dege, I say.

What does that mean?

It doesn't, I reply.

"I'm one of the nicest guys in the world."

I raise an eyebrow. If a man ever tells you that he is the nicest guy in the world, he is probably a psychopath.

"No, I'm really nice."

I nod. We keep rolling. Like many drunks, he repeats many of the same things over and over. "I have a boat! I own a beautiful boat and I'm rich."

He asks for a cigarette. I tell him I'm out.

"Well, pull over and we'll buy some."

OK.

I pull up to a convenience store, walk in, and buy a pack. I give him two.

"Oh, god. I love you. I really need this," he says while lighting the cigarette. I nod. No problem.

He is happy. Drunk and happy. And supposedly rich, with a boat. He slowly leans over to me as if he's preparing to give counsel on a very serious subject.

"I'm not gay. But if I were to give someone a blowjob. I think it would be you."

OK, buddy.

"I've never done that before in my life."

I raise an eyebrow, and then as an afterthought, I tell him I'm straight.

"Fuck you. I'm not gay," he says. "Daniel Flaherty is not gay."

Of course you're not, I say. Relax. I tune him out for a bit.

"I'm still fucking rich."

We arrive at his two-story, brick house. Nice place. The fare is ten dollars. He reaches into his wallet and pulls out a ten-dollar bill. And then he makes a showy display of tipping me a dollar as if he's bequeathing to me the golden keys to the secret kingdom.

Have a good night, buddy.

I roll out of there, thinking Daniel Flaherty may not be gay, but he is very kooky.

THE LEPER OF ST. FRANCIS MOTEL

Pick up at the charity hospital. My passenger is very thin, and his hands are shaking.

"I've got AIDS. I'm dying," he volunteers as we pull into traffic. He holds five bottles of prescription medicine. They rattle around in a Ziploc bag.

He is living at the St. Francis Motel, which is the worst motel in town. Murders, drug deals, prostitution, rats, robberies, you name it. It all goes on at the St. Francis Motel.

During his day, the real Saint Francis dressed in rags, served the sick as well as lepers, preached in the streets, lived in poverty, and was disinherited by his father.

We drive along in silence. I watch him stare at the world whipping by the window like a slideshow.

Street after street.

Block after block.

"I don't know how long I'll be here."

His days are stamped with a number,
    just like mine,
    just like all of ours,
        except he happens to know
        more so than the rest of us
        the manner in which the end will come.

THE TRAITEUR

Pick up at apartment complex. I roll up. An old man is waiting outside. Age: early seventies. He is dressed in a peculiar suit like a salesman from the 1940s. He sits up front. He says he's hungry and wants to go to a restaurant. He seems like an interesting guy.

"My name is Fred Roy!"

There is something weird about him, but it is a cool, harmless weirdness. He talks about casinos and gambling. He really wants to go gambling tonight. But he isn't sure if he can afford the cab fare. His brain skips around like a broken record.

"Where's Cankton? You ever been to Cankton? I got kin there."

Cankton is north of Lafayette.

"I want to go to Cankton and gamble. I like to gamble! But I can't afford it."

I nod. We arrive at the restaurant. I drop him off. An hour later, he calls for me to pick him up. I return to the restaurant.

Where to? I ask. Cankton?

"No, I can't afford Cankton. Just take me home," says Fred.

OK.

Out of curiosity, I call my friend Colby, who happens to live in the same apartment complex as Fred Roy. The phone rings, and Colby answers.

You ever been to Cankton? I ask Colby.

Fred interjects, "YES, HE HAS!"

I laugh. I ask Colby if he knows Fred Roy.

He does.

"Fred is a traiteur," says Colby. A traiteur is a Cajun faith healer who combines Catholic prayer and medicinal remedies to heal people.

We pull up to Fred's apartment complex. I am intrigued by this traiteur thing. Before Fred leaves, I ask him about it.

"It's a gift," he says, gazing wistfully into the distance. That's all he says. It's a gift.

I ask him if he will work his magic on me.

"What is hurting you?"

I say that physically, I am fine, but throughout my life I have experienced other things that have scarred me emotionally.

He nods pensively.

"My daddy beat me too."

Fred exits the cab.

"I'll be right back. I have to grab something."

Fred goes into his apartment and then comes back to the cab.

"Lay back and relax," he tells me.

I do. He puts his hands on my head and begins to pray. It's a strange feeling. The sensation is Tuscan-cool with electric yo-yos of light telecommunicating from my eyes, in concentric rings that play ping-pong games with the soul formations on another world.

Actually, that didn't happen.

But I did feel a mild sense of peace as he put his hands on me and prayed. I hope it helps. I'm not sure if anything will change. Fred Roy seems like a good soul.

When he is finished praying over me, Fred remains quiet for a minute. I thank him and roll off into the night. He stands in the dark, watching me leave. He smiles and waves until I can't see him anymore.

And I drive away.

Hopefully into a new life.

FANFARE

Rainy night on the shift.
I fly down the alleyways
And buckling boulevards
As the rain sizzles upon the pavement
And the tilted masts of power lines
Slant like sinking ships,
Accelerating
Block after block,
Ghetto to ghetto.
I sweep past the strobe of streetlights
As the police sirens sing out,
Echoing above
Burnt bulbs, billboards, and neon,
Bathed in the barbed wire skyline,
Feeding us the false hope
To dream and delude ourselves
For another payday,
Like a fanfare of things
That have come before us
But may never come again.

CRAZY EIGHT

Pickup: a trailer park.
Female, midforties.
She walks out of her trailer
Dressed like Raggedy Ann.
She sits up front, wearing a bright red wig,
Lipstick,
Patch-quilt dress.
At first,
I assume she is going to a costume party.
But I am wrong.
She's just crazy.
This is who she is.
This is how she dresses.
She informs me her nickname is "Crazy Eight."
"I'm Marylyn Monroe today."
Where to?
She gives me the address.
We listen to jazz on the radio
And roll through the streets.
She talks with a lisp.
Plays with her wig.
Stares into space.
She tells me she once
Snorted a menthol cigarette.
Why'd you do that?
"I was bored."
What did it do?
"It made me crazy," she says.

CRACK DADDY

Pick up at a midtown apartment. Roll up. Honk. Wait. Five minutes pass. I honk again. Finally, they appear in the parking lot. A dad, mom, and a baby. Dad's about forty-five years old, an offshore-worker type.

Where are we going?

"I'll direct you."

He won't give me a street, just some vague directions on the north side of town. He's got a sketchy vibe. It's 11 p.m. on a Wednesday. I figure they are making a late-night trip to the store for diapers or something.

"You cool?" he asks.

Uh, yeah, I guess so.

"You ain't a cop, huh?"

I shake my head. No.

Sigh.

"You cool?" he asks again.

This guy is already annoying me. He leans forward.

"I'm trying to score."

I roll my eyes.

Why'd you bring your family along?

No reply.

I inform him that I don't think this is a good idea and that I'll just bring them back to their apartment. Crack Daddy gets angry and raises his voice. I raise mine. I tell him if he doesn't shut up, he'll be walking home.

"Not without my wife!"

I clarify that his wife and kid are fine, but I'll leave his sorry ass out here. He stews on that for a bit and then points to a gas station.

"Stop here. I want to buy smokes."

I pull in. He hops out and disappears in the dark behind the building.

I ask his wife why she tolerates it.

"He supports the two of us," she says. "I don't mind him doing it, as long as he can pay bills."

Crack Daddy returns. His demeanor is noticeably different. Now he is eager to return home. He must have scored his drugs in the parking lot. I shake my head, press the accelerator, and drive them home.

Their problems are nothing I can fix.

They'll have to fix it themselves.

Or maybe not.

THE LOSERS

I'm dispatched a call to pick up two white boys in the hood. They're standing on a corner when I arrive. I pull up. They hop in. They want to go to a trailer outside of town. I call in to get an estimate on the fare from the dispatcher—twenty-one dollars. I turn around to collect the fare in advance because these guys are a little sketchy and I suspect they'll run on me. They look disheartened.

"We ain't got no money."

Sigh.

I state the facts. If they run on me when we arrive at their destination, I will have to pay their fare. They shrug. I can see they're just hapless fools. And I want to help them. But they are a risk. We discuss the situation. Each of them attempts to convince me of their good intentions.

Here's what we are going to do, I tell them. Give me your IDs. I'll hold them until we get to their destination and I get paid. Will that work for you guys?

"Yes."

They hand me their IDs. I remind them that I am doing them the favor, not vice versa. We roll.

What were y'all doing out here in the middle of the hood?

"We just got robbed."

Is that right?

They proceed to give the details.

"We are from Michigan."

They met two Louisiana girls online and moved here a year ago.

"We all live in a trailer now."

The girls turned out to be crazy.

"Now we're stuck down here."

Tonight, the dudes were bored and decided to get in their car, come to town, and grab a few beers. They hit some bars. They had a good time.

"It felt good to be away from our crazy girlfriends."

They drank their fill and then started heading home.

As they were driving down the road, a woman ran a red light and smashed her car into them. The cops came. They both failed the DUI breath tests. So did the old lady. But strangely, the cops let them all off with tickets. No DUIs.

"Got lucky, I guess."

Their dead car was towed away. They tried to hitchhike home. But no one would stop to pick them up. As they were standing on the corner, some thugs walked up and allegedly robbed them. They had no other options, so they called a cab. And that's where I enter their story.

So here we are.

We roll, IDs on the seats, losers in the back. We make the twenty-minute drive to their trailer. When we arrive, they go inside. I wait.

One of the crazy girlfriends comes out and pays me.

I give her their IDs and we all live happily ever after.

LOVERS' QUARREL

2:14 a.m. Got a call to pick up at a house near the college campus. I roll up. Honk. Wait. Honk again. Wait. I rest my eyes for a few minutes.

Suddenly, I hear a screen door kick open. Two men exit the house, an older guy and a younger guy. They argue in the front yard. Loudly. I watch them curiously. I'm guessing that these are the guys who called for the cab. The younger guy is dressed only in tighty-whitey underwear and is bleeding from the nose. The older man is heavier and fully clothed.

"I want you to leave, now!" says Old Guy to Young Guy. Young Guy paces around in the yard. He does not want to leave.

Old Guy repeatedly tells him to leave.

Young guy screams at him, "You know I can't do that!"

Young Guy dances around in the yard. Drunk and confused. I roll down the window.

Which one of you guys called the cab?

Old Guy steps up.

"I'm a professor at UL. He is one of my students. He's drunk and doesn't want to leave. I called the cab for him. I'll pay for it. If he doesn't leave, I'm going to call the police."

Fair enough.

I yell over at Young Guy: Hey! Show's over, buddy. Grab your pants. Your friend wants you to leave.

He pauses.

Come on. Let's get out of here.

He ignores me.

Young guy does not seem to realize his nose is bloody and that he's in his underwear. He's oblivious. Old Guy looks at me.

"Please get him out of here."

I can't make him do something he doesn't want to do.

Young Guy looks at me and points at Old Guy.

"He's a Jew!"

Young Guy does a little hand-dance like he's shining a shoe in the air. I light a cigarette and let this play out. Young Guy runs off behind the house. Old Guy pulls out his cell phone.

"I'm calling the police."

Do what you got to do.

Young Guy returns carrying a cat and jumps in the back seat of the cab.

"Let's go!" he yells.

"Put the cat down!" says Old Guy.

"No! It's my cat! I gave it to you."

Young guy jumps out of the cab and runs back into the house with the cat. He returns a few minutes later, carrying his clothes and no cat.

"The police are on their way," says Old Guy.

"Fuck you!" Young Guy gets back in the cab. "OK, let's go."

Old Guy gives me twenty dollars.

"Get him out of here."

We roll out.

At a red light up the street, Young Guy jumps out of the cab, carrying his clothes and runs back in the direction of Old Guy's house. I let it be. My job is done. They'll figure it out.

THE SPEED OF LIGHT

The night slows.
The shift eases into a meditative blur.
I am alone.
I coast through the streets
Past wilting signs
Towing neon.
I watch them glaze over the windshield
Between pranks of the wind.
I look inside myself.
I look outside at the world.
I try to make sense of it all.
I don't know if I ever will.
But I keep going onward
With the illusion of forward progress,
     Rising in volume
          Like a flat line.

HORROR AND HALLELUJAH

3:44 a.m. Pick up in a residential neighborhood. Roll up. Honk. Out comes a lady wearing pajamas and a robe. Approximately forty-five years old. Hair ragged. Circles around her eyes. She appears tired, weary.

Where do you want to go?

"The north side."

It's kind of late. You mind if I ask why?

"Pills."

OK.

"I was in a car accident two years ago."

We roll through the darkness to an old house across town near the railroad tracks. We pull up. Ghosts and drug addicts mill about the front yard. They stare at us, jumpy and paranoid. She is unfazed. She exits the cab in pajamas, robe, and slippers. She makes small talk with the addicts and disappears into the house. When she comes out, she hands drugs to two of the crackheads and then jumps back in the cab.

We roll out. She lays down in the back seat, in a dreamy reverie.

"I'm killing the pain."

She repeats this like a mantra over and over.

KILL THE PAIN.

She is safe now.

Resting inside the church of her own soul,
> Among the shadows and tolling bells,
> Somewhere between the horrors and the hallelujahs
> Of this world.

DEAD MAN MOTEL

Pick up at the charity hospital. The passenger is a petite, black woman in her midforties. Her name is Ruby. She is very nervous and edgy.

What's wrong?

"I saw a man get shot."

Where at?

"St. Francis Motel."

Did he die?

"Oh, yeah."

What happened?

Ruby was hanging out with the dead man at the motel. Dead Man was a construction worker with a good job and a work truck. He wanted to party. They got a room and bought a lot of crack. They smoked all the crack and then ran out of money. In exchange for more crack, Dead Man "rented" his truck to a dope dealer for a few hours.

The dealer left and was gone for two days in the truck.

They continued smoking crack and hustling money to buy more crack. Finally, the dealer returned to the motel with the truck. Dead Man and the dealer argued. One of the dealer's friends pulled a gun. He shot Dead Man in the chest.

Everyone ran out of the motel room. Dead Man died, high and alone.

The police arrived and questioned everyone. They knew that Ruby was involved. They took her into custody. She played dumb. They took her to the hospital for a psychiatric examination. She continued to play dumb for twenty-four hours until she was finally released.

This is where I meet her.

We roll back to the St. Francis Motel where all of her stuff is. I drop her off. She pays the fare and walks back into the night.

NEVER FORGET

Pick up at the charity hospital. It's an old man in a wheelchair. I help him into the cab, fold up his wheelchair, and put it in the trunk.

"I drove a cab in New Orleans for nineteen years," he says.

He is a Hurricane Katrina evacuee. During the storm, he was stranded in an old folk's home.

"They flew me out on a helicopter. Off the roof."

We roll back toward the housing project where he lives. He is hungry. But he has no money on him. He asks me if I can buy him some food.

"I'll pay you back," he offers.

Don't worry about it. What do you want to eat?

"Fried chicken."

We pull into a drive-thru and I buy him some fried chicken.

He eats and we roll onward.

We arrive at the projects. I help him out of the cab and into his wheelchair. I push him up the hill to his apartment. He hands me the keys to his place. I open the door and roll him in. His place is barely furnished, almost empty. In the corner, I see some old jazz records and a stereo. The TV is on.

He digs around in a bag hidden under the couch and pulls out some money and pays for the fare and the fried chicken. I give it back to him.

Don't worry about it.

"I appreciate that."

I ask if he needs anything else.

"No, I think I'll be OK."

We say our goodbyes.

"Just don't forget about me," he says as I walk out the door.

I won't.

THIRD WORLD AMERICA

What a brutal world we live in.
The violence.
The drugs.
The frenetic pace.
This is the wasteland.
Come suffer with us
 Through all the games that power plays.
 We will break you
 Just as we have been broken
 In the cycle of destroying one another.
Come step into the haunted house
 Of our Third World American Dream.
Here are the cockroaches.
Here is the absent father.
Here are the holes in the walls.
Here is the broken glass.
There is the shadow of the older brother
 Drugging himself into the next life.
Here are the bills.
 Slave tickets.
And here are the children,
 Playing amongst it all,
 Incredibly resilient,
 Unbreakable for the moment.
Fire up the blast furnace
So that we can incinerate ourselves
 Quietly in the low-income order
 Of dead cars
 And slave wages
 Shuttled about on the city bus,
 In the taxicab,
 Through the subway,
 In the alleyway along the boulevard.
Thank your president

And the power brokers
And the programs
That were put in place to enslave us
Again
And again.
You can choose your poison here.
Make it your drink of choice.
It's on the house.
We're giving it to you.
It's Happy Hour on the suicide watch.
Smash the bottle over your head.
Pose for the mugshot.
You've earned your place
In the Palace of Enslavement.
Clock-in at the prisons and factories.
    They want you
    For the war effort.
Come on in and spin the wheel.
Win the lotto.
We'll make it fun.
You can dream.
You can hope.
But we make the rules.
And only we win.
Until you wake up.
And quit blaming one another.
We want you to hate one another.
We will layer lie upon lie
And you will believe them all.
We will broadcast the lie
    Into your living room.
    And you will believe it.
    You will live it.
    And you will learn to love it.
    You will love it more than your own family.
    And when that power betrays you,
    You will accept it.
We will keep you segregated.
And dumb.

Pointing fingers
And placing blame.
Go on, do it.
It's what you're good at: being a victim.
The white will hate the black.
The black will hate the white.
The Hispanic will hate the both of you.
    As will the Asian and Arab.
None of you will know,
    Aside from a few,
    Who we are
    And what we are.
We want war.
We want you to fight our wars.
Our own children will not fight these wars.
Instead, they will own you.
And you will never know
    That you are owned.
You will be too busy
Looking for someone
Within striking distance
    To blame
    And victimize.
    You will be our victim.
    You will in turn,
    Victimize your own children.
This is our way.
You will follow orders.
You will obey us,
And you will never know
The truth of it all,
Even if the truth be told,
    Because you will not believe it.

HOOYAH

2:31 a.m. Pick up at a bar. The passenger is an Iraq War veteran. This guy is a piece of work. Drunk. Very combative and difficult. Just back from Afghanistan. He wants to get more alcohol. I tell him everything closes at 2 a.m. He gets angry. I tell him to relax. I explain there is an after-hours bar in the next town. It is twenty minutes away. We can legally buy alcohol there.

Do you want to go? It's a twenty-five-dollar fare.

He haggles about the price of the trip. I stop the cab. The price is set. Either we go or we don't.

"OK, let's go! But it better be right."

I roll my eyes. Right as what?

We roll.

You can tell this guy's head is fucked up from the war. He's just not right. He's wired too tight. The conversation is sparse and tense. When we arrive at the bar, the place is packed. I walk in with him. He looks uncomfortable here. He wants a fifth of whiskey and a case of beer.

I try to help him get the attention of the bartender. We stand at the crowded bar as country music blares. The guy wanders off. He stands in a corner and stares aggressively at the locals. I walk over to him, lead him back to the bar. We order from a bartender. The bartender sells him whiskey and beer and bags it up. I grab the stuff and turn to exit.

Now the guy is off in a corner, talking to the locals. It looks as if they are arguing. I cut into the middle of the group and launch into a quick speech about how this guy recently got back from Iraq and is very stressed out. To their credit, the locals immediately relax. Now they want to buy him a drink. So, we all do a round of shots. Everybody's happy.

We roll out.

On the drive home, he thanks me.

He's not a bad guy.

He's just crazy

    And like the rest of us

    He cannot figure out why.

CHRISTMAS IN A BLACK HOLE

Christmas Eve on the night shift. I am dispatched a call to pick up south of Broussard, Louisiana. South of nowhere. It takes me twenty minutes to find the residence. I drive down a long dirt road, past country shacks and fields, until I locate a dilapidated trailer.

I pull up. Honk.

Out walks an old man with a beer. It's cold, dark, the wind is blowing. Dogs are barking somewhere. He climbs in.

Where to?

"My nephew's trailer in Maurice."

It's twenty miles away.

"They are having a little get-together over there."

He smells like old farts and burlap. His name is Johnny Cadeaux. We shake hands. He's drunk. Drunk people love shaking hands. After the tenth handshake, I just start throwing an elbow toward them. They usually understand. Not Johnny Cadeaux, though. He gets pissed when I give him my elbow in place of an actual handshake.

"You son of a bitch! You too good to shake hands with Johnny Cadeaux?!"

Sigh.

To appease him, I shake his hand a few more times. We take some shortcuts down the backroads through the winter night. We stop at a convenience store. He buys beer, whiskey, and cigarettes. He insists I drink a beer with him.

Thanks, but no thanks. I can't drink and drive on the job.

He's a crusty old fart, but he's real. He was married four times. Has six kids. Worked seventy-two jobs. Owned five different houses. Made all kinds of money. Lost it all. Now he lives in an old trailer alone.

"I like to drink whiskey and play the accordion."

We roll on toward his nephew's trailer. It's located on an isolated country road. When we arrive, the lights are out. Johnny climbs out of the cab and makes his way through the dark to the door. He knocks. It's a polite, but plaintive knock.

No answer.

He knocks louder, balling his fist and beating on the door.

Nothing.

The cold, icy wind blows around us.

Silence.

Johnny yells at the door.

"Come on, you motherfucker! You brought me all the way out here to drink? And now you ain't even going to answer the door?"

He picks up a potted plant and throws it at the side of the trailer. It rattles with a thunderous boom. Apparently, no one is home. Just the wind and the cold. Johnny turns, defeated. He walks slowly back to the cab and climbs in. With an agonizing grunt, he shuts the door.

"Take me home."

We roll back.

Johnny is quiet. We fly down the darkened back roads toward his house. Chattering valves, engine rumbling. He makes us both a drink. He passes me a cup. I take a tiny sip to appease him. The volume of his voice rises back to full mast.

"It's a good night to be alive!"

By default, I have become Johnny's drinking partner. We blow down the gravel roads. Johnny talks. He gives me advice.

"Never get married."

OK.

"Buy land."

OK.

"Don't trust a man who dances better than a woman."

OK. Duly noted.

"Never go into business with a man who complains a lot."

I like that one. I nod at each directive.

We roll on. We laugh. We talk. At one point, we stop to piss in the fields. He yells at a gang of cows in the moonlight.

"Get on out of here, cows!"

We keep rolling. After a few more twists and turns, we arrive back at Johnny's trailer. It's been a good ride. Johnny pays the fare. I say my goodbyes, but old Johnny does not want me to leave. He insists I come in and have one more drink. I try to talk my way out of it, but he's not having it.

"Come on, it's Christmas Eve. I'm all alone."

Sigh. This is true.

It's kind of a slow night, so I opt to go into his house for a few minutes. I climb out and walk to his trailer. The interior looks like a bomb went off. Old stuff everywhere: work clothes, car parts, board games, ancient tools, weathered newspapers, dead TVs. He points at a TV and lowers his voice as if giving me some secret wisdom of the ages.

"I never turn them off."

We sit. He talks about his family, his sons, his daughters, and his ex-wives. "They don't come around no more," he says. "It's just me out here."

Well, you got me now, Johnny.

"That's better than nothing," he laughs.

Merry Christmas, I say.

"Ça c'est bon."

It's just the two of us sitting in a junked-out trailer, spinning round the galaxy in the middle of a field somewhere in Louisiana. It's a lonely kind of Christmas. Johnny reaches into a box and pulls out an old accordion. He proudly shows it to me and then begins to play. I sip my drink and listen. He squeezes the accordion of all its ancient dust and fleas. It's got a darkened wheeze.

Johnny breaks into the saddest, most out-of-tune, brokenhearted version of "Silent Night" I've ever heard in my life. Johnny squeezes out that song in the dim pinball machine of his ragged trailer, among the towers of junk and debris. It's tragic and perfect in its own way. It almost makes me cry. He finishes with a mighty squash of the bellows.

The silence swirls around us. We continue to drink and talk and laugh until the clock arms slide down the wall and I notice the time is late.

I have to leave. I don't want to go, but I have to.

I nod and stand.

We hug as strangers
> who have shared a nice moment
> in the middle of nowhere
> in a trailer sitting on the edge of the world
> where old dogs get tossed out
> and a new breed comes in to eat them alive.

CLOTHED IN FLESH

Christmas on the night shift.
I drive through the cold streets
Listening to classical music
Wondering
Waiting
Moving through this world
So sad and sweet
Maybe even holy
Just ringing
And singing out
Like a bright light shining
Through a body of water
Slowing moving
Into the next moment
But there are no dates
Nor days
Nor holidays
Or years
Just the ever-present moment
With your soul clothed in flesh
Where you look out
Upon the fabric of this world
And see
And listen
And wonder
If it is all real
Or if it even matters
Perhaps there is no real or unreal
Just illusions
Shuffling in the shadows
Whispering with the ghosts of this world
In series
And number
And program

And stock
With our hearts made of ash
Abandoned in smoke
It doesn't have to be real
Or unreal
Just a sense
Of something more vital
Than what has come before
As we climb
Midway up a staircase
Of piano keys
Marked only
By the elasticity
Of our own flesh
As it grows lower
And closer to the earth
Nudging us further along
Past the good graces
Of each lighthouse
And into the darkness
Of the good night.

Q-TIPS

Pick up at a hotel. Passenger is a male, late fifties.
"I'm retiring."
He is from Flagstaff and on his way to Miami.
"I'm going to party and live out the rest of my days."
That's his plan.
I ask him why not stay in Flagstaff?
"Too many Q-tips!"
What are Q-tips?
"Old people like me."

BEASTS OF A SORT

Pick up at a shack on the north side. My passenger's name is Brandi. She's a prostitute and a drug addict. She literally lives in a lawnmower shed behind some guy's house in the ghetto. When I pull up and honk, she slides open the door and walks out of the shed.

She is thirty-five but looks fifty. Fifteen years ago, she was probably beautiful. She tells me she won nine beauty pageants when she was a teenager; her grandmother pushed her into it.

Now she's addicted to crack and has been on the streets for years.

Prostituting herself

Going to jail

Smoking crack

Getting beat up

Repeat

I've picked her up in the cab many times over the past few years. She was one of my first fares. Now here she is. Here we both are, three years down the line, both of us a little worn out. But she is tougher than I will ever be. She is a Goliath of survival and I am her witness.

I drop her off at the motel. I watch her walk away like an animal through the jungle.

I can't even judge her

Or the way she makes her money

Or lives her life

Or kills the pain.

I can't judge her because we are all beasts of a sort.

Chapter 4
NOWHERESVILLE

THE GREAT DIVIDE

My skin is pale.
My eyes are dark.
I am tunneling through the night
In this yellow submarine of a cab.
The parade of people,
The train of images
Projected through the windows.
The accelerating faces and colors of humanity,
Screaming past.
Night and day, rolling over
Like illusions
Birthed in a puzzle of numbers
Dressed up as facts.
I robotically grind through the motions
Of each night's shift
    Coming.
        Going.
           Speeding.
              Turning.
                Slowing.
                  Stopping.
The endless procession
Pickled in neon and night.
I push onward into the bubble of the windshield
With each second's passing,
As the hours tug
At the flesh of my face
And my heart flinches
And curls up
Inside its warm shell
Surrounded by the massive gulf of night
Stretched out and yawning,
Bottomless and infinite,
Leaving me to wonder,
How will I cross that great divide?
And make sense of it
With only word or number.

THE WAY OF THE GUN

Full moon. Monday night. It's a very slow shift. For the first half of the shift, I make the usual run of calls. Around 10:30 p.m. there is another lull in the shift. Typical for Monday nights, which are usually slow. I park downtown by the Greyhound station. I talk shop with the other drivers who are parked there as well.

Fifteen minutes later, I get a call from the dispatcher:

"Pick up at the Oak Trace Apartments, #33."

Oak Trace is a totally bombed-out apartment complex in the ghetto. Dark. A little unpredictable.

I take the call and roll out. The destination is in the rear of the complex. I pull up. Four dudes are standing outside in the parking lot. They flag me down. They appear to range in age from seventeen to twenty-four years old. They want to go to Ile Des Cannes, that small ghetto on the other side of town. Sixteen-dollar fare.

They all pile in, three in the back and one in the front. The guy sitting up front seems to be their leader. His front teeth are capped in gold with some initials stamped in them. I'll call him Goldie.

"We're going to a house party to meet some girls."

I nod. As I'm pulling away from the building, Goldie asks me to stop.

"I got to grab something real quick."

OK.

I stop the cab. He steps out and walks off. We sit in the parking lot, waiting for him. The guy sitting directly behind me steps out of the cab and stands slightly behind my door, which seems strange, but I don't think much of it. Goldie returns and hops back in the front seat.

Before I can put the cab back in gear, Goldie pulls out a chrome-plated revolver and points it in my face.

"THIS IS A JACK!!" Goldie yells.

I am being robbed.

One of the guys sitting behind me reaches up, kills the ignition, and tosses the keys on the floor of the cab. The guy that was standing outside pulls open my door and stands there.

"Where the money?" yells Goldie.

They had me fooled. I stay calm. All I see is the barrel of the gun about twelve inches away, aimed at my head. Just like in a fucking movie, my eyes focus solely on the barrel of the gun. It's a big black hole staring me down. My heart speeds, but I don't panic. My hands don't even shake. I just laugh and shake my head. What else am I going to do?

Just be cool, I tell Goldie.

I slowly pull out the sixty-one dollars in fares I've collected for the evening.

That's all I've got. You want it? There it is, I say.

Someone behind grabs it out of my hand. Goldie is to my right, half in, half out of the cab with his door open. He is still holding the gun in my face and erratically shaking it.

"Where's the rest?!" he asks.

I don't know.

The other dudes scramble around the perimeter of the cab, offering support like some cheerleading robbery squad.

"Jack him!"

"Get that money!"

"Where's the rest of the cash?!"

"Where's the rest?!" Goldie yells.

That's it, I say. That is all I got. It's a slow Monday night. That's all there is.

We have a stand-off where they repeatedly yell "Where's the rest?!" and I keep replying that is all there is. It's a weird feeling, having a gun pointed at your face by someone who is robbing you. You don't know if they have it in them to kill you. I wait for the sound of the gunshot and the lights of this life to go dark.

As I stare at the black hole in the barrel of the gun, I can feel my consciousness peeking over the wall of sleep and looking down into the darkness of the next world. I glance over at Goldie. He's jumpy. I keep waiting, sitting there, on the ledge between this world and whatever awaits me in the next.

And then, just as quickly as it began, it ends. As if on cue, they all run off like schoolgirls into the darkness. I grab my pistol from under the seat, where I keep it stashed for situations such as this, which I've never before had reason to use.

I hop out of the cab and rack one in the chamber. I look around. My focus switches from one guy to another as they all run off into the darkness between apartment buildings. I see one of them climbing a fence. I aim my gun at him.

Then I pause. Catch my breath.

Thinking.

I could try to shoot at any of these guys. Put a bullet in them. But there's also the possibility I could miss and hit someone else. Maybe a baby in a nearby apartment or someone else. Maybe a single mom, cooking dinner for her kids.

I shake my head.

This is so dumb.

It's just money. Sixty-one dollars.

I put the gun back under the seat.

Sigh.

I climb back in the cab, slowly put it in gear, and roll out. The night is quiet.

I grab the radio and call in the "emergency code" to the dispatcher: 10-6. This informs the dispatcher that there's been a serious incident and I need police assistance. In five years, this is only the second time I've had to do that.

The dispatcher immediately answers.

"You OK?"

10-4.

The banal, numerical language of the CB radio code conceals the tension and weight of the previous ten minutes. It's just numbers. Numbers like smoke signals that signify some condition in this life. The economy of the code—so efficient, like an airstrike.

"Where are you parked at, Driver Four?" asks the dispatcher.

I inform him of my location, so that he can relay it to the police.

"Sit tight, Number Four. I'll send them your way."

10-4.

I park two blocks away in a vacant parking lot near an elementary school. Two squad cars arrive within ten minutes. I step out of the cab to meet them. One of the officers is dressed in black tactical gear and uniform with a bulletproof vest and an automatic weapon.

To begin, I describe the robbery, the suspects, the apartment complex where it happened. A few more squad cars appear. They drive through the apartment complex and the surrounding neighborhood looking for the suspects. I fill out a police report. One officer gives me a number to call to check on the progress of the case and drive off.

I climb back in the cab and complete the remainder of the shift. It's a long, slow night.

Periodically, I glance up at the moon through the canopy of clouds and wonder if I am still here, alive in this world, or dead in another that looks just like this one.

THE ONE-ARMED MAN, PT. 3

I'm dispatched to pick-up at a working-class, redneck bar. I roll up. Honk. No one comes out. I honk again. No response.

I kill the cab and walk in the bar. I head straight to the bartender and ask who called for the cab. The bartender looks around and points to a guy leaning against a pillar.

"That's him."

I turn. It's the One-Armed Man, smoking and shooting pool with some regulars. I approach and let him know I'm here.

"Not you again," he says.

Tonight, he is wearing a full-length prosthetic arm in place of his missing arm. It's made of plastic with a metal hook and pincher on the end.

"I've got to finish my game. Then we can go."

I nod. I sit on a barstool and wait, watching him navigate the table. For a guy with only one arm, he's actually pretty good at shooting pool. He finishes the game. I'm not sure if he won or lost. I wasn't that invested in it the specifics of the outcome, but more so his dexterity with the new prosthetic arm. I walk toward the door. He slowly follows. As we exit the bar, he raises his new prosthetic arm in the air.

"How do you like my new toy?"

It looks good, I say.

He is obviously still getting acclimated to the new device. The mounting straps are a little loose and hang off the side of his torso, causing the prosthetic arm to swing chaotically from side to side like a broken chicken wing.

We climb in the cab. As usual, he sits up front.

We roll.

He directs me to his house. I remind him I know where he lives now.

"Keep it a secret."

I nod.

"I don't like people knowing my business."

Do you remember me from our last ride together? I ask.

"I can't get involved with all you cabdrivers. You're all the same."

I laugh to myself.

"Stop at the store. I need cigarettes."

We detour to the nearest convenience store. He climbs out and struts into the store. His new arm knocks against the entrance and swings wildly back and forth, straps flowing like streamers at his side. A man follows him into the store and takes a cautious step back. One-Armed Man buys his cigarettes and exits.

We roll on.

I pull up to the One-Armed Man's house. It's the same place where I watched him fall into a ditch and accidentally light his hair on fire during our last ride. This time he climbs out of the cab with no disasters.

Good job, I tell him.

"Fuck off!" he says.

You got it. Have a good night.

He pays, waves, and walks off. There's something about this guy. I don't know what it is. Although he is disagreeable and grouchy, there is still something likable about the One-Armed Man.

THE CRAZY WIFE

Pick up: a rangy trailer park. The place is full of dead cars, shredded trailers, piles of trash. As I'm dodging the massive craters that pepper the access road around the place, I search for trailer #65, but as is the case with many of these places, most of them have no address numbers on the sides.

As I go up and down the rows, honking in the dark, a man flags me down from the shadows. He's a big man, six-foot-five, and he looks scared. A woman follows him.

The man jumps into the back seat. As he attempts to close the door, the woman gives chase and blocks the door with her body.

"So this is it? You leaving? You just going to go like that?" she screams. The man does not acknowledge her.

"Let's get out of here, man," he says to me. She begins throwing several punches at his head. He wearily raises his arm and shoulder to block the blows. He pushes her back and tries to close the door. She blocks it, again.

I tell her to calm down and step away from the cab.

No response.

When she finally pauses to catch her breath, I press the accelerator and pull the cab forward. The open door swings wildly.

"You motherfucker!" she screams, while running alongside the cab.

We roll through another cratered street and the door bounces shut. I pull further away. In the distance, I can hear her cussing at us both. He has made his escape. The cab bounces through one last crater and we lurch into traffic.

"Can I get a cigarette?" he asks. I toss him one and a lighter.

"Thanks for getting me out of there."

Are you all right?

"Yeah, that bitch is crazy."

Who is she?

"My wife."

THE RUNNER

Call to pick up at Edison Street. I have always had bad luck on this street. I pull up. Guy in his midtwenties walks out, jumps in the back seat.

We roll.

He's going to a neighborhood on the other side of town. He gives me vague directions—not a specific address, just some cross streets on the other side of town. When we arrive, he points to a house and asks me to stop.

"I got to run inside and get the money."

He hops out, walks up to the house, and then ducks a fence and disappears.

FUCK! I had a feeling he was going to run. I don't even bother to chase him. Fuck it.

I throw the cab in gear. Roll around the hood, look for him. Of course, he's long gone. He's probably already sitting on his couch watching TV and eating popcorn. Motherfucker. I hate getting burned. You lose a little faith in humanity every time you get burned.

I return to the shift, running calls for the next hour.

At some point, later in the shift, I am back in the neighborhood where I picked up the guy who ran on me. I see a full garbage can sitting on the curb. I roll down the window and grab the can with one hand and drag it up the street alongside the cab. It makes a god-awful noise.

I pull up to the address where I picked the runner up.

I step out and hurl the loaded garbage can toward the house. It bounces into the yard and tips over. I don't know if that was his house or just someone he knew. I don't even care. I'm weary and tired and don't give a fuck anymore. I now understand how cops become assholes on the job. After years of dealing with the same idiots, the same fuck-ups over and over, you lose some hope along the way, and you realize you really can't change the world. You can't even dent it.

And on a night like this, all you can do is drag a garbage can around a shithole neighborhood and hope nobody sees you.

I know it's petty. And stupid.

But that's the only solution I have left in me.

MOMMY'S GOT A HANGOVER

Pick up in the projects.
Single white mom comes out.
Three kids.
Mom's a mess.
Hair like a nest.
She and the kids climb in the cab.
"I've got a hangover."
OK. Where to?
"Walmart."
We roll.
The kids sit quietly in the back.
The mother asks if I can turn down the radio.
"I got a hangover," she tells me again.
I turn it off.
One of the kids leans over to the mom.
"Don't get drunk tonight, Mommy. Just drink Coke."

TEXAS

I'm parked at a gas station, idly waiting for the next call. An old black man approaches the cab.

He's drunk.

Possibly crazy.

Babbling, stumbling.

He knocks on my window. I roll it down. Shredded tobacco leaves are stuck to his lips, as if someone smashed a cigar into his face. He lowers his head toward me.

"I'm from Texas."

THE OKIES

Call to pick up at a gas station near I-10. As I roll up, I see a tow truck, a minivan, and a family of four standing nearby. Mother, father, son, daughter, and two dogs.

"We're from Oklahoma," the father says. "Our van died."

Dad has long hair, a beard, and tattoos. Mom's got a beer gut bigger than Dad's and a mouth full of Corn Nuts. Everyone is dusty and dirty, but polite. They're salt of the earth folks. "We've been driving for two days. It finally up and died."

It's like a scene from *The Grapes of Wrath* meets Dairy Queen. It's depressing. They drove here from Oklahoma to vacation in post-Katrina New Orleans.

Hey, honey, let's grab the kids and the dogs and drive down to New Orleans in your brother's piece-of-shit minivan. Yeah, the one that spits black smoke out of the tailpipe. That's the one. We can get drunk and walk around and the kids will have a blast.

Well, at least they've got gumption. That gumption thing goes a long way in getting you from Point A to Point B when you are used to going nowhere. It breaks my heart to see people so desperate and stranded without a clue and with their two kids and two dogs. The son even has a pet lizard in the back seat. No bullshit. I overhear Dad mention it to Mom as we unload their van.

"Don't forget the lizard!"

I love America. I really do. But it ain't easy.

We load the Okies and all their stuff in the cab and then we roll. They want to go to a hotel. So, I bring them to a hotel. Dad goes into the office, while the rest of them wait in the cab.

Then Dad comes out. Their bad luck has struck again. The hotel will not rent them a room.

Why?

"We don't have a credit card."

Ouch.

At this point, I just want to give up, pack it in, and join their Okie family. I can't just leave them here, so I might as well go all the way—join up with them and become part of the clan. I'll stake out a spot in the back of the minivan and sleep between the two dogs, the beer cooler, and the pet lizard.

That'll be my spot. "Oh, don't mind him. That's just cousin Dege," they'll say.

We sit in the parking lot of the hotel and debate their options.

Homeless shelter? Another motel? Sleep in the minivan at the garage where it is being fixed?

I roll my eyes.

To hell with it. I'll get you a room, I say.

I walk in and put their room on my credit card. Damn Okies. Them and their bad luck will break your heart. I walk into the office and get them a room for one night. I walk out and hand them the room keys.

"Thank you so much!" The Okies are so happy and thankful that someone has taken pity on them in the middle of this shitstorm of bad luck. The only religion I have is helping people. I may as well put it into practice.

We unload their stuff. I say my goodbyes and give them my phone number in case they run into any other problems. I climb in the cab and roll out, trying not to think about the fate of those sweet Okies and the sad people of the forgotten American Dream.

BREAKING & ENTERING

2:15 a.m. Friday night. The bars are closing. I swing through downtown.

A drunk couple flags me down. They are sitting on a curb. It's a pretty blonde woman and an athletic, yuppie guy. I'll refer to them as Barbie and Ken. They are both in their early thirties. I wave them over. They both drunkenly scissor-step toward the cab, wasted. They climb in the back seat.

We roll.

Where to?

Ken wants me to bring them to his place.

"No, I want to go home," says Barbie.

They argue a bit in the back seat, trying to figure it out. Apparently, Ken is trying to score with Barbie, and Barbie just wants to go to sleep. They must be in the early courtship stage. As they debate their destination, I roll in the general direction that they are going, which is a neighborhood named River Ranch.

I stop at a red light. The argument in the back seat rises in intensity.

"Fuck you!" yells Barbie. She suddenly opens the door, exits the cab, and walks up the street toward a mini shopping mall.

I'm not sure what to do.

The light turns green.

Cars honk behind me.

I ask the guy what he wants to do.

"Leave her."

You're not going to go get her?

"No, she's not worth it," he says.

Class act. I hesitate, look back. I see Barbie walking off. I make a mental note of the area and the direction that she is headed. I will come back and get her. Ken is not bothered. His soul is like a flat tire. He doesn't give a shit. Ken's house is only a mile up the road. I haul ass, running a few red lights, and quickly drop him off.

"How much?"

Ten dollars.

He pays. No tip. Again, class act.

I roll out of there and speed up the road toward Barbie and the area where I last saw her. Upon arrival, I search around the mini mall. Where are you, Barbie girl?

I check the parking lot. No Barbie.

I check the back alley. No Barbie.

I swing by some nearby store fronts. No Barbie.

No, wait. There she is. She is standing in front of a closed trophy shop, looking lost. I beep the horn and yell toward her.

"Hey! Let's go!"

Right on cue, she turns and drunkenly scissor-steps toward the cab with no fuss and no argument. She hops into the back seat. I ask for her address, but her speech is slurred and I can't understand her.

"Elysian Fields . . ." she mumbles.

What?

"500 block."

Close enough. We roll through the night. Immediately, she lies down in the back seat and tries to go to sleep.

Please, don't go to sleep, I say. You can't go to sleep on me.

I give the steering wheel a few shakes to roust her. You can never let the females fall asleep in your cab. You can never let anyone fall asleep in your cab. It's just too much trouble. It usually results in the driver not getting paid for the fare, because you can't touch them to wake them. They could accuse you of rape or sexual assault or something like that. It's always better to simply keep them awake.

How do I get myself into this shit?

I shake the steering wheel a few more times.

Hey, wake up!

But it's no use. She sits up for a minute and then passes out. I roll my eyes. This is not going to be easy. I locate her street and park on the corner of the 500 block.

We sit there, cab idling.

Wake up, ma'am!

No response.

I honk the horn. Hard.

No response.

I turn up the FM radio. Loud.

No response.

She's still sleeping. No movement. No nothing. Pause. Think.

I hop out, walk around, open her door. She's sleeping on her side. Hands folded beneath her head. I grab a stick from beneath a tree and tap her on the shoulder with it.

Come on ma'am. Wake up, please!

I get no response. Nothing.

I tap her again with the stick. It doesn't work.

Pause.

I put my hands on the seat near her head and I bounce the seat up and down several times while yelling, HEY, WAKE UP! She opens her eyes. That worked.

Come on! Keep coming! Wake it up. Wake it up!

"Whaaaaat? Where am I?" she asks.

I'm your cabdriver. I'm trying to get you home. What's your address?

"I can't remember."

We're on your street. Come on. Take a look around.

"It's Elysian Drive."

That's where we're at, sweetheart.

She swats her hand in the air like I'm bothering her. I bounce the seat cushion, again. Her head jostles up and down.

Come on. Let's go.

I have a plan. My plan is to walk her up and down her street until she recognizes her house.

Come on, let's walk, I tell her.

She sits up. I help her climb out of the cab. Barbie holds my arm as she drunkenly makes her way up the block. I steer her to the sidewalk. As we pass each house, I point and ask, is this your house?

"No, I don't think that's it."

We walk to the next. Is this one your house?

"No. That's not it."

Next. Is this it?

"That house is ugly."

I'm starting to lose faith in the plan. We continue to the next house. Pointing. Is this your house?

"No."

Do any of these houses look familiar?

She points to a house up the street. "I think that's it."

We walk up to it. She looks around, confused. Shakes her head.

"No, this isn't it. It's the next one," she says.

Are you sure?

"Yes!" she yells.

We walk to the next house and go to the front door. We stand there, looking at one another. Silence. She's confused.

"Where are my keys?" she asks.

189

Keys? How the fuck should I know? I'm just your cabdriver.

She pats down her pockets. No keys.

"Where's my fucking purse?"

How should I know? I don't remember you carrying a purse.

"Fuck! Where the fuck is my phone?"

Phone? Keys?

"Where's all my stuff?!"

I roll my eyes. She must've lost all her shit in the drunken blur of the evening. Man, these yuppie women really cut loose.

Maybe your boyfriend has them? I suggest.

"Fuck him!"

We stand there in silence.

I can't leave her out here, alone on the street. Maybe I can break into her house.

Come with me, I say

I walk around her house, checking to see if any of her windows are unlocked. We walk around to each of them, but unfortunately, they're all locked. Of course they are. She jerks my arm.

"Hey, we can get in through the backdoor."

OK! Show me where it's at.

She leads me around to the back of the house. But her fence gate is locked. She claws at the fence in a drunken attempt to climb it. I pull her away from the fence.

Look, I'll climb over and unlock it. Wait here.

"OK."

I climb the fence and hop over. Then I unlatch the lock and pull the gate open. She walks in. We're in the backyard. A crime light pops on and bathes the backyard in a harsh light. There's a swimming pool, a courtyard area, patio furniture, a large barbeque pit, garden tools, and kids' toys everywhere.

She leads me to the back door. It's a set of double doors. I turn the knobs. Both are locked. I shake my head. Barbie plops down in a patio chair.

"I give up."

I check the back doors again and give them a measured tug to see how far they'll open. They've got some play in them. It may be possible to just pop them open. She notices what I'm doing.

"Just break it. I've got to get in my house."

I give the doors a couple hard tugs and on the third pull, the doors pop open. Boom. Thank God.

Come on, I say.

Barbie stumbles across the patio and into the plush arena of her living room. It's a nice place. Really nice. Giant flat-screen TV. Expensive furniture.

Barbie dumps herself on the couch. She's home. She's safe.

My job is almost done here. I tell her the price of the fare: fifteen dollars. She stares at me quizzically.

"I don't have any money. I don't even have my purse!"

Oh yeah. I forgot.

OK, well I guess I'll just pay your fare.

"Fine. Whatever works." I turn to leave and say goodnight.

"Hey, aren't you going to get my number?!" Number? Now I'm confused. What is she talking about?

"You're going to leave and not even ask me for my phone number?!" She's angry now.

"You dick!" she yells.

It's at this point that I realize she's so drunk, she thinks that I'm her date. What the fuck is wrong with these people?

You really are drunk, I say. And you're probably not going to remember any of this in the morning. I'm your cabdriver. I drove you home and we broke into your house.

She's laying sprawled across the couch. She's not even listening to me. That's my cue. I turn to leave and let myself out the front door, carefully locking it behind me. I walk up the street to where I left the cab. I jump in and roll the fuck out of there.

It's 3:53 a.m.

I finish out the remainder of the shift, running two more calls, and then I drive toward the cabstand. What a night. As I drive, I review the strange details of the evening.

As I'm doing this, I suddenly remember Barbie's lost purse. I pull the cab over, stop, and reach behind the seat. I feel around, and then I find it lying on the floor. Her keys, wallet, credit cards, cell phone, and other crap are all inside. All of it.

I drive back to Barbie's house and place the purse behind a plant on her porch.

I also leave a note on her door.

You probably won't remember any of this, But I'm the cabdriver who drove you home last night. You lost your purse along with your keys and I helped you break into your house. After I dropped you off, I found your purse in the back of the cab. I left it behind the plant on your porch. If you'd like to pay for the cab fare ($15) or have any questions, you can call me here. 337-XXX-XXXX. —Dege

And with that, I roll out.

The next day, she does not call.

THE DILDO

Pick up: a prostitute going to a hotel.
We roll.
How's it going tonight? I ask her.
"Going to meet a customer," she says. "He likes toys."
She giggles.
I feel something tap me on the shoulder.
I turned around.
It's a foot-long dildo, waving in my face.

THE PUKERS

2 a.m. I'm trolling downtown as the bars close. A group of twenty-some-things flag me down. They're drunk. Not just drunk, they're wasted and ob-noxious. And like most drunks, they are loud.

They pile in, all five of them. We roll toward a mid-city residence. A few miles into the ride, the guy to my right rolls down the window.

"I've got to puke!"

He begins to gag. I slow the cab and switch lanes to pull over. Before I can stop, he sticks his head out the window and begins to puke. Most of it goes out the window. The rest of it splatters on the passengers in the back seat.

Suddenly, the guy's sister, who is sitting directly behind him, begins to gag. I immediately power down her window. She sticks her head out and they both puke into the night.

Finally, I stop the cab. They both exit and puke together on the side of the road.

The other passengers moan and groan.

I do a bit of groaning myself,

Seeing as how I'll be the one who will have to clean it up.

WIDE LOAD

12:33 a.m. Call to pick up at a house where some regular customers host a card game. It's a women's bridge club. They play every Wednesday night.

"What cab are you driving?" the dispatcher asks.

Strange question, I think. He's never asked me that before.

Cab #34. Why?

"OK. Just checking. That cab will do."

I roll to the address. Honk.

From the house, three enormous women emerge. They walk toward the cab. They are big girls, each of them weighs approximately 300–400 lbs. With a series of grunts and groans, the women wedge themselves into their chosen seats in the cab. One up front, two in the back.

At first, I don't think much about it: their combined weight, that is. But as each of them climb in, I notice the buoyancy of the cab's suspension sinks dramatically.

Whoa. This might not be good.

I can actually feel the stomach of the woman sitting behind me, pushing up against the back of my seat. In addition, the tummy of the woman sitting up front almost touches the dashboard.

They're going to Breaux Bridge, Louisiana, twelve miles away. I cautiously put the cab in gear and roll out. It becomes immediately obvious that this will not be a normal cab ride. As we traverse the route, the cab moans, buckles, and strains under the combined weight of the women. With each bump and dip in the road, the rear of the cab bottoms out on the wheel wells. Each bump in the road is announced with the horrifying scrape and squeal of metal and rubber, thunderously grinding.

OH MY GOD.

I try to remain composed and professional as the cab's shock absorbers squeak, twist, and squeal. No one in the cab laughs or even makes the slightest hint of acknowledging the situation. I've never had this happen before. But then again, I've never driven three 400 lb. women home.

I ease the cab up the road and attempt to find a speed that lessens the stress and the bottoming out. I try driving painfully slow and also exceedingly fast, but nothing works. So, I resign myself to an uncomfortable fifteen-minute drive to their destination as the cab bumps, scrapes, and grinds along in the night. My eyes and mouth are wide for the entirety of the ride.

As we progress, the sound of the cab bottoming out becomes more pronounced and violent. I try to ignore it and stare straight ahead. As we pass a man walking on the road, I study his reaction to our passing in the rear-view mirror in order to gauge how badly the car might be sagging. But there is no indication that there is anything unusual.

The ladies play it cool and talk amongst themselves. They're delightfully oblivious, which actually makes the entire ordeal easier to deal with. The cab's suspension announces each corner as we navigate a dozen agonizing turns through the city of Breaux Bridge.

We finally reach our destination.

Thank God.

I drop them off. As they exit, the cab quickly snaps back to its proper elevation.

They pay the fare.

I politely thank them and roll back to Lafayette in silence with an odd look on my face.

THE ONE-ARMED MAN, PT. 4

Call to pick up at a neighborhood bar in an industrial area. I roll up. Honk. No one comes out.

I kill the cab and walk in. The bar has a varied clientele. It caters to everyone from the laborers to debutante queens to yuppies and barflies. I nod to the locals and make my way through the crowd. I locate the bartender and inquire as to who called the cab.

She points toward the pool tables.

I look in that direction.

There he is, again: the One-Armed Man.

Just like the last time I picked him up, he is shooting pool. And once again, he is wearing his new prosthetic arm. I walk over and let him know I'm here.

"Hang on a minute," he says with a dismissive wave of his hand. "I'm shooting a game."

What a character. Prince of the Prosthesis. I wish I had the creative talent required to make a guy like this up. He's too real. And he's unintentionally funny. I stand aside and observe him. As I noted the last time, he is a pretty good pool player. With each shot, he adroitly balances the stick on the pincher of the prosthetic arm and takes aim. He makes about half of the shots and actually wins the game. The man he is playing hands him some money. They shake hands.

The One-Armed Man nods to me, indicating he is now ready to leave. We exit the bar. But first he has to piss. He ducks into an alley and relieves himself. When he returns, he sits in his usual spot: the front passenger seat.

"Just a heads up. I hid my money under a garbage can behind the bar."

Why did you do that?

"So if I get robbed, I won't have that much money on me. Don't let me forget it."

How much did you hide?

"Ninety-two dollars."

What kind of scumbag robs a guy with one arm? I ask.

He gives me a knowing and troubled look.

"You'd be surprised."

We roll out.

Where to?

"My girlfriend's house down the road," he says. "But I want you to wait for me there."

I nod.

We roll in silence and arrive at the woman's residence. The One-Armed Man exits the cab and goes inside his girlfriend's house. I wait outside and read a book to kill time.

Thirty minutes later, he appears in the yard, puffing on a cigarette. The One-Armed Man makes his way toward the cab, bobbing, weaving, stumbling. He is considerably drunker than he was when he entered the house. His usually immaculate haircut is frazzled and messy. It looks like someone rubbed his head down with a car wash rag. His body leans at an odd angle as he walks toward the cab, tripping over a plant along the way before magically righting himself. His prosthetic arm wildly gesticulates as if conducting its own symphony or snapping beatnik-like to passages of complicated jazz music.

He stumbles left, then wide right. Wobbles a bit. Gathers himself and then sloppily trudges forward in fit of chaotic steps that result in him lurching against the side of the cab. Exhausted, he tugs the open the door and plops down in the front seat. Mission accomplished.

Where to?

"Home. I can't do it anymore."

Do what?

"Just drive!"

We roll out. As I navigate traffic and turns, he sloshes about the interior of the cab, cursing my driving, women, and liquor. As I make a sharp right turn, his body tips over and almost falls into my lap. I stiff-arm him back to an upright position. He doesn't like that.

"Don't touch me!" he yells. "And slow down!"

Take it easy, cowboy. I'm just trying to get you home.

"I'm drunk!" he yells angrily.

I know, man.

"Well, then drive *right*."

I shake my head and offer no reply. He looks pale. Paler and drunker than usual. Let me know if you have to puke, I tell him.

"I never puke!" he says.

Good man.

"You're working with a pro."

I appreciate that in a passenger.

197

Suddenly, the One-Armed Man braces himself with the dashboard.

"STOP!" he says.

What is it now?

"I forgot my fucking money!"

What money?

"The money I hid at the bar!"

Oh, yeah. That money.

"Under the garbage can!"

What do you want me to do?

"We have to go back and get it."

Sigh.

I turn the cab around and steer us in the direction of the bar. We roll through the empty streets. He lights a cigarette and rolls down a window, swaying back and forth in the front seat. We arrive at the bar. It is closed.

"I'm too drunk to get up," he says. "You go get it. It's under the last garbage can."

OK.

"And it better all be there!"

I roll my eyes and exit the cab. I walk into the alley where he pissed and hid the money. I see three garbage cans. I kick the third can over and see his wad of cash on the ground. Fifty-two dollars balled up and soiled. I grab it.

When I return to the cab, the One-Armed Man is half asleep. I toss him the money.

"It better all be here."

What if it isn't?

"Who would steal from a guy with one arm?" he asks.

You'd be surprised, I say. He gives me a knowing nod.

"You're goddamn right!"

We roll out.

I drive him home, leaving him to his lot.

Just as I am left to mine.

NO WIVES, NO DEBTS, OR PETS

Pick up at a bowling alley. My passenger is a male in his midsixties. He's fun and talkative, cracking jokes, laughing. I ask him, what's the secret to being happy?

"To what?"

To living a happy, fulfilling life?

"No wives, no debts, and no pets!" he exclaims.

I laugh.

"Every day of my life has been great, because of a lack of those three things."

I tell him he should add "no regrets," since it rhymes.

He looks at me quizzically.

"Oh, I've got regrets," he says. "Just no wives, debts, or pets."

BILBO

Call to pick up at a grocery store. It's a lady with a ton of groceries—three carts full of groceries to be exact. I load them into the cab. When we arrive at her apartment, I unload them all again.

"Can you help me bring them in?"

Yes.

As I carry the groceries into her apartment, she tells me to keep the door shut.

"So the rabbit won't get out."

Rabbit?

She points to a corner of the room. I don't see anything.

"Look under the chair."

I turn and see a little rabbit, staring straight at me. Just sitting there, watching. I call to him.

Hey, buddy.

He does not move. He stares at me, motionless.

What's his name?

"Bilbo."

THE WHIZZINATOR

Pick up: South Point Apartments. A dude in his early twenties hops in. Where are we going?

"The head shop."

We roll.

You in the market for a new bong?

"No, I'm applying for a new job and I have to pass a piss test tomorrow."

Oh.

"I got fired from my old job," he says.

We roll in silence. The guy is bummed out—just sitting there, ruminating on his ruminations.

Why'd you get fired? I ask.

"I was working for an oilfield company." During a twelve-hour lull between shifts, he tells me, he and a coworker borrowed a company truck.

"Drove it four hours to meet some girls."

They went to the bar. They got drunk. Somewhere in the night, they wrecked the truck. To cover their asses, they abandoned the truck and reported it stolen.

"Nobody believed us."

They both got fired the next day.

"My parents were pissed."

He knows he fucked up.

"I have to fix this. I got an interview tomorrow for a new job."

But now, he's also got another problem.

"I smoke weed every day and I can't stop."

Now he has to flush it out of his body in order to pass the drug screen. I nod. That makes sense.

We pull up to the head shop. The door is locked. 9:58 p.m. He knocks on the door. The people inside can see him, but they inform him that they are definitely closed and will not reopen the store for him at this time. The kid returns to the cab, dejected. I mention another head shop across town. He brightens up.

"Let's go!"

We speed across town and quickly arrive at the other drug paraphernalia store. Surprisingly, it's open. He goes in. I wait. He soon returns carrying a bag.

How'd it go?

"Not good, but I think it'll work."

What did you buy?

"They were out of detox tea," he says. "So they sold me this."

He pulls out an insane contraption that looks like a strap-on dildo attached to a diaper and syringe.

What the fuck is that?

"It's called a Whizzinator."

It's a crazy little contraption.

"It better work. It cost me eighty dollars."

We examine the contents. It contains a fake penis, rubber bladder, and urine injector. It even includes a hand warmer to heat up the urine so it mimics body temperature. Very strange.

"I hope it works."

You don't have much choice, I tell him.

"No, I don't."

We roll out.

I drop him off at his apartment. He is happy. There is a spritely pep in his step as he walks away with the Whizzinator, swinging around at his side in the plastic bag. This could be the beginning of a great chapter in his life or just another wrong turn down an endless maze of cold dead ends.

A STRIPPER NAMED ANGEL

2:10 a.m. Pick up at a strip club. A blonde female exits the locale. Her name is Angel. She's a stripper and a regular customer in the cabs.

Where to?

"I've got a little job lined up."

OK.

"A customer wants to hang out for a bit."

OK.

"Do a little business."

We roll to an apartment on the south side of town.

"I don't know this guy," she says. "So, I'm a little nervous." She hands me a piece of paper with his phone number on it. "If I'm not back in twenty minutes, call this number. Tell him you are waiting outside," she says.

OK.

We arrive at the destination. I park the cab.

"Most of these guys only last five to ten minutes. So don't go far."

She exits the cab and walks up a set of stairs. The night is quiet. I settle in. Read my book. Listen to the radio. After twenty minutes, there is no sign of Angel.

Let's give this a try.

I call the number. A man answers.

"Hello?"

I'm outside waiting for Angel, I tell him.

"She's coming out right now, sir."

Sir? That was professional. Sure enough, a door opens and out walks Angel. Hair disheveled. She hops in the cab.

You all good?

"Yes. That guy knew how to fuck."

We roll out.

How much did you make?

"$150."

She tips me twenty dollars.

We roll toward her apartment.

"Can you do me one more favor?"

What is it?

"Can you walk me to my door?" she asks. "My boyfriend is very jealous."

Why is he jealous?

"He thinks I fuck around on him."

I nod.

"He knows you're the cabdriver. He'll think I came straight from work."

Whatever you say.

We arrive at her apartment. I walk her to the door. As we round the corner to her apartment, her boyfriend is waiting there to meet us. He's a big dude and looks pissed off. He eyes me suspiciously.

"Who's this?" he asks.

"He's the cabdriver," says Angel.

Hi.

I turn and roll out, avoiding all eye contact.

Because my eyes never lie.

MAD DOG 20/20

Call to pick up way out in the country. Nowheresville. Scarcely a mailbox every two miles. After much frustration, I locate the house and pull in the driveway. Honk. Out comes a midthirties, nerdy-looking guy dressed in sneakers and stained sweatpants.

Where to?

"A liquor store."

I inform him the nearest store is twenty miles away.

"It doesn't matter."

OK.

We roll.

What are you drinking?

"Mad Dog 20/20."

Good enough, I say. It's forty dollars to the store and forty dollars back, I inform him. Eighty dollars total.

"That's fine."

Why spend eighty dollars just to get some cheap liquor? I ask.

"It's my birthday."

HOPE IS THE ONLY ESCAPE

Pick up at a small house in the ghetto. Black lady and her teenage son. They are going to the bank. They sit in the back seat and calculate figures as to how to pay this month's bills. It is moving to see them work as a team.

Tough times.

Struggling in the American ghetto.

There are no vacations to exotic places.

The only escape is hope
    And the wishbone,
    Snapping one way or the other
    Above the August bells,
    Ringing with the spit and clang of ancient prayers.
The jigsaw checkerboard houses, warped and sinking,
The overgrowth of the subtropics,
    Pulling everything back down into the dirt
    As the concrete rises again to smother the earth.
    Along with the broken bottles of shattered stained glass
    Cupped at the foot of stone and iron,
    Courtrooms and barnyards,
    Prisons and skyscrapers.
    Sometimes you just want to burn it all down
    Because the deck is so stacked
    And the odds so long
    That the only language left to speak is one of violence,
    Violence that seems to say:
        Let us humble those who have humbled us.

We pull into the bank drive-thru and wait our turn at the altar. They feed their money into the tube. It disappears. The teller talks over the speaker. There is a problem with the check. The woman talks into the speaker, the speaker talks back. Somehow, the problem is resolved. The tube comes back with money in it and a receipt. Transaction complete.

We roll and I drop them off at their house. It's a crumbling shotgun shack, indistinguishable from the others. They pay their fare, and I roll.

Ten minutes later, I find a checkbook on the floor of the back seat. I open it up. I look at the address on a check. It's the same people I just dropped off. I spin the cab around and speed through the ghetto.

I pull up in front of her house. I see the woman standing outside, anxiety-ridden, almost in tears, searching the yard, the gutters, and streets. Her eyes beam like twin lighthouses in a sea of madness. I roll down the window and hand her the checkbook. She squeezes it in her hands, quietly sobbing.

"Thank you," she says. "Thank you so much." She holds my hand, not wanting to let it go.

It'll be OK, I say.

At least I hope it will.

A MAN CALLED PIE

Pick up at the charity hospital. I roll up to the ER. Pump the horn. In the corner of my eye, I see a nurse pushing a man in a wheelchair. I hop out of the cab to help them. The man is a double amputee. His left foot is gone below the knee and the right is about the same, freshly amputated and bandaged. Two nubs.

The nurse and I help him into the front seat. The newly bandaged leg has dried blood on it. I turn to grab the wheelchair and load it into the trunk, but the nurse rolls it away from me.

"This belongs to the hospital," she says.

That brings up an interesting question, namely: How is this man going to get out of the cab and into his house?

Maybe he uses crutches, I think.

But how? He has no feet! Fuck it. I'll figure it out when we get there.

We roll. He's a sweet old guy. His name is Pie. He is in his midsixties with a beautiful grey Afro. Skinny frame. Deep, soulful eyes.

What happened, Mr. Pie? I ask.

"Diabetes," he says. "It took my other leg, too."

Are they always so businesslike at the hospital?

"They're cold-blooded sometimes," he says. "But I don't fault them."

What a keeper this guy is. At least this world hasn't taken his heart. Yet.

We plow through the sunshine and afternoon traffic. He stares out the window, daydreaming, smiling. The wind races around us. He's simply enjoying it for what it is. It's so easy to get caught up thinking about all the things we don't have. I am guilty of doing this as well. It can make you bitter. But then you meet a guy like Pie. He's got no feet, no ability to walk, and yet he's happy and content to enjoy the ride. Some people just have that something special that gets them through the hard shit.

"Boy, you sure know how to drive," he says.

Yes, sir. Thank you.

We pull up to Pie's house. It's an old shotgun shack in the hood, right by the railroad tracks. Many others just like it on each side. His front yard is overgrown.

"Grass done got high," says Pie. "I been in that hospital for two weeks."

As I'm parking the cab, I remember that we don't have a wheelchair for Pie.

How are we going to do this, Pie? How do I get you in the house? I ask.

"I got an old wheelchair inside," he says.

He hands me his keys.

"You go inside, grab it, bring it back here."

I like a man with a plan.

I unlock his house. It is clean and well organized. Old pictures of family adorn the walls. Grandmothers. Kids. Brothers. Sisters. Cousins. Grandkids. His wheelchair is in a corner of the living room, sitting there, waiting for him like an old dog.

I roll it out.

Pie sees me, sits up, and readies himself to exit. Both of his amputated limbs poke out from the open door. I reach in, lift him like a child, and place him in the wheelchair.

"You good?"

Pie nods.

"Don't forget my bag."

I grab his bag from the trunk and push him up the walkway to his house. He motions for me to stop.

What's up, Pie?

"I want to sit outside," he says. "And enjoy the sunshine for a little bit."

Wow. I marvel at him.

He's like Diogenes of the ghetto
>But even more resilient
>and mythic
>and most importantly, humble.

STUCK INSIDE OF MOBILE

1:05 a.m. Saturday night, slow shift. The dispatcher calls me on the radio. "Are you awake enough to drive to Alabama?"

I guess so. Why?

"We just got a call going to Mobile. You want it?"

I calculate the drive and return time. I think about it and realize that if I take the call, I will not get back to Lafayette until noon the next day. Fuck it.

Let's go. I'll take it, I tell him.

He gives an address to pick up in Crowley, Louisiana. I grab a coffee at a gas station and mentally prepare myself for a long night.

I roll to the pick-up location. It's a small house. I pull in the driveway. Honk. A door swings open. Out comes an older white guy in his late sixties. He is walking on aluminum canes and dragging a bag. I hop out and help him load in. He hands me $400, which is the cost of the fare. Paid in advance. Nice. It's great when people do that.

He sits up front. We roll out, heading down I-10 East. I set the cruise control at 75 mph.

Three hours and forty-six minutes to Mobile.

The passenger's name is Max. He had planned on taking a Greyhound bus to Mobile, but he missed the last departure at midnight, so he called a cab. He is going to visit relatives in Mobile.

"My brother and his wife live there," he says. "Good people."

Max is kind of spacey.

"I don't drive," he says. "I get too stressed out."

He may have Alzheimer's disease or an old head injury. I'm not sure what it is. But he is coherent and conversational. He's has a boyish face for an older man.

"I was raised by my mother. I still live in her house."

Max likes to talk about music, movies, and Jesus. Especially Jesus.

"Jesus helps me every day," he exclaims.

Rolling along. An hour into our trip, Max falls asleep. Every now and then, he slumps over toward me and I have to nudge him back over with an elbow. I maintain alertness by chain smoking and listening to Art Bell on the radio. I crank down the windows and let the cool night air circulate through the cab.

Somewhere in Mississippi I run over something in the road and the right rear tire goes flat. I steer the cab to the shoulder of the road and stop on the side of I-10. I pop the trunk, grab the tools, and jack up the cab. Traffic whips by me, ripping massive blasts of wind. As I change the tire, a state trooper pulls up behind me. He kicks on his police lights to warn oncoming traffic away. That's nice. I appreciate that. I give him a nod and a wave of the hand.

Max sleeps through the whole thing. As I lower the jack, I can see his head bounce and wiggle with the movement of the chassis. I finish up, thank the trooper, and roll out. We plow through miles of night and eventually arrive in Mobile just before dawn.

I shake Max by the shoulder.

Wake up, buddy. We're here.

"Where?"

Mobile, Alabama. I need the address of your brother's house.

For some reason, I'd forgotten to ask Max the address when we left Crowley. I think I got distracted when he handed me four crisp $100 dollar bills.

So, what's the address, Max?

"Uh . . . it's off of Hillcrest."

What? Where the hell is Hillcrest?

"I'm not from Mobile. I don't know."

You don't know? Oh, shit. Max, you've got to have the address somewhere.

"I know generally about where it is," he says.

Well, you're going to have to *generally* help me find it.

I can't believe I just drove two states away without asking him for a specific address. What a dumb move. In addition, Max does not have a cell phone and cannot remember his brother's phone number. I should've noted all this before we even left his driveway.

OK. How am I going to do this? With no specific address, I've got to rely on Max's memory to locate his brother's house. This will be interesting.

As we roll into Mobile, the light of dawn turns into the slate grey of morning. We enter the tunnel that goes under Mobile Bay. Sensing the unfamiliarity of the tunnel, Max announces, "We've gone too far!"

OK. I exit, turn around, and head back toward West Mobile. Max stares out of the window, scanning the city like a lost little boy. He mutters the name of each road sign we pass.

"Government Street, Spring Hill Ave, Hooper Road."

Where are we going, Max? Help me out.

"What do you want me to do?"

What is your gut telling you? I ask.

"Take the Downtown exit," he says.

OK. That's good. We're getting somewhere. I flip the blinker and make a hard exit into downtown. I find myself talking to Max as I would a child.

Come on, buddy. You can do it, Max.

"This doesn't feel right."

OK. It doesn't feel right. That's OK. Let's see what it feels like if we go in another direction. I turn the cab north.

OK, Max?

We drive through another section of the city.

"None of this looks familiar."

I pull the cab over. Stop.

OK, Max. What else do you remember about your brother's house?

"It's near an airport, a bus station, and a church."

OK, that helps. That's good.

I scan the map, locate the airport, and drive in that direction.

Stay with me Max. Keep alert.

Max and I spend the next hour zooming around neighborhoods near the airport. The early morning streets twist and coil around us. It's as if the city of Mobile is a Ouija board and Max is my psychic divining rod. Needless to say, it is very confusing and difficult. But that's all I've got.

We turn onto a tree-lined boulevard.

"This feels familiar."

Yes! That's good, Max! Which way should we go?

He points west.

"That way."

OK. I drive west. And if he points east, I drive east. That's how we do it. As we progress through the interior of Mobile, Max begins to recognize landmarks.

"I know that donut shop!" he says.

That's good, Max! That is *good.*

We drive through neighborhoods near the donut shop but find nothing. Max's antenna goes dead and we are lost again.

Stuck inside of Mobile with the Max blues again.

Frustrated, I pull up to a Waffle House and ask the waitress if there is a bus station around here. She gives me vague directions and name drops some local landmarks, none of which I am familiar with. It's actually more confusing than helpful. But she does mention a bus station. It's around here somewhere. But somewhere could be anywhere.

I climb back in the cab and double check the map.

"How'd it go?" asks Max.

Not good, but we'll be alright. Think positive, Max.

We roll on. I return to the process of conjuring the Ouija board of Max's mind. I ask him to look for landmarks, houses, grocery stores, churches, anything that might trigger his memory.

"Just think of Jesus and we'll get there," says Max.

OK, buddy, I will. I roll my eyes and shake my head. You never know, maybe Jesus will help.

"Keep thinking of Jesus," he says again.

Now Max is Ouija-boarding my mind! With Jesus.

We drive on.

How are we doing, Max?

"Go that way." He points straight ahead.

OK.

We start getting into another section of Mobile with very different scenery than downtown area. Giant oak trees. Old, stately homes.

At this point, I'm starting to worry that we will not find his brother's house. What am I going to do? Drive back to Louisiana with him? It's not looking good. But then a strange thing happens. The further we get into Mobile, the more landmarks Max begins to recognize.

"I know this road. This looks very familiar."

Fantastic! What do you see, Max? Where do we go? Just tell me what to do, buddy.

"I just thought of a street: Shady Lane!"

OK, that's good! In fact, that is great! Where is Shady Lane?

"I have no idea."

I moan and pull the cab into a parking lot. Stop. I check the map and search for Shady Lane, but I am unable to find it.

"Keep thinking of Jesus and we'll find it," he announces again.

At least Max has faith.

Is Shady Lane the street your brother lives on? Or is that the name of their neighborhood?

"I don't know. Try that way," says Max, pointing in a random direction.

Having nothing else to go on, I simply follow the direction of Max's finger.

We roll on.

We enter a residential neighborhood. Max goes blank. In an attempt to jog his memory, I call out street names as we pass them.

Southridge!

"No."

Hillcrest!

"No."

Quail Creek!

"I got nothing."

Think of your Jesus, Max. Where does he want you to go?

"Maybe he doesn't love us."

Oh, he loves you, Max. Jesus loves the shit out of you. Stay with me.

We drive aimlessly up and down a few more residential streets. Then we hit a dead end. Max goes completely blank. Nothing. We backtrack. Max is silent.

Talk to me, buddy. Where are we going, Max? What do you see?

"I'm thinking of Jesus," he says. "And so should you."

I pound my chest with a fist. I got Jesus right here, buddy.

We roll on. Aimlessly. Suddenly Max points to a sign.

"Look! Shady Lane!" he screams.

And sure enough, there is a street sign: SHADY LANE.

Yes! Thank God! I yell out.

"Thank Jesus!" he says.

Yes! Thank Jesus! He's helping us, Max. The street leads into another residential area.

"We're close, I can feel it," says Max.

YES!

Max points when he recognizes a house.

"I know that house!"

Good, Max!

He recognizes another house, and another.

"I know that house, too!"

We're going to make it, I think.

"Turn on the next street," says Max. "I think I know where we are."

You do?

"Yes," he says confidently.

Fantastic!

I turn right.

Max sits up in his seat and points.

"That's it! I think that is my brother's house!"

Max, are you sure?

"Yes!"

Thank God.

"Thank Jesus!" he screams.

I pull into the driveway and beep the horn. Out comes an older gentle-man who looks just like Max.

"That's my brother."

Yes. I pat Max on the back. Yes! We did it.

Max's brother approaches the cab and greets us. They hug. I unload Max's bag. It's a joyous occasion. Everybody's happy. Max is happy. His brother is happy. I am happy. What a relief.

I say my goodbyes and climb back in the cab to leave. Then I realize, with all the driving and searching and Ouija-boarding of Max's mind, I have no idea where the fuck I am.

I roll down the window and motion to Max's brother.

How do I get out of here? I ask.

Before he can answer, Max interrupts us.

"Just go back the way you came," says Max. "And think of Jesus."

THE CAN MAN

Early morning.
5:22 a.m.
The streets are flat as an old hooker's ass.
And empty.
I am still on the clock, working.
I see a homeless man in the street.
He is pushing a shopping cart
And rooting through a dumpster.
Scavenging.
I watch him.
He's stoic and resolute.
He tosses cans into his cart.
He sees me watching him.
We lock eyes.
He gives me a friendly wave.
Any man who can traffic in this world,
In the manner he does,
And is without hate or bitterness,
Rightly deserves all this world
Has refused to give him.

THE DRUG SMUGGLER

My passenger is a male in his midfifties. His name is Jim. We talk. He's from Florida, He's in town visiting his father, who is sick and in the hospital.

"Where's the weed?" he asks.

I don't know. I don't smoke.

"I was a drug smuggler," he says. "Back in the day."

How'd that do you?

"Not too good in the end."

How'd you smuggle the drugs in?

"I'd drive a van with a hollowed-out roof. Pack it with weed and coke."

Is that right?

"They'd rivet the roof shut and seal the drugs in."

Then, he said, he'd drive from Mexico to the U.S. He'd cross the border in Brownsville, Texas.

"But sometimes I'd cross in Laredo."

He would then drive up to Chicago.

"Eventually, I got busted."

How?

"Somebody tipped them off," he says. "Probably a DEA informant."

He had 120 kilos.

"I did ten years in a federal pen."

Did the DEA try to get you to rat out your suppliers?

"Yes. But if I would've talked, I'd be dead."

OX

Friday night. 2:52 a.m.

I get a "police call," which is when the police call for a cab. Usually, the cab is for someone they take pity on who has been in an accident or something like that.

The address is near Fraternity Row. I arrive on the scene and see three patrol cars. Lights on. Nearby, a car sits in a ditch. My passenger is in the back of a police car. The cops take him out and lead him to the cab. He climbs in and gives me his address.

He is a college student, early twenties. His name is Ox.

We roll.

What the hell happened? I ask. He tells me the story.

Ox went out with his buddies to drink and meet some girls. They got really drunk. By the end of the night, no one had met any girls. Then the bars closed.

On the drive home, they saw some pretty girls in a car next to them. They tried to get the girls' attention. The girls drove off. The guys drunkenly followed them for the next fifteen minutes. They tried to signal the girls to stop, so that they could talk and hang out. Instead, the girls called 911 and reported that they were being followed by strange men.

Within minutes, a cop pulled up behind them. The driver tried to lose the cops. The cops gave chase. While attempting to flee the cops, they crashed the car in a ditch. Everybody piled out of the car and ran in separate directions. Everyone but Ox.

Why didn't you run?

"I was drunk and passed out in the back seat."

Wow.

"I slept through the whole thing," he says. "All I remember is waking up and seeing four cops pointing guns at me."

THE BIKER

Call to pick up at an assisted-living community. My passenger is a long-haired biker in a wheelchair. He looks like a roadie for the Allman Brothers Band. His leg has been amputated at the knee.

I hop out and help him into the cab, pack his wheelchair in the trunk.

Where to?

"The store."

He wants beer and cigarettes.

We roll.

I ask about his leg.

What happened?

"I hit a car and woke up six months later."

CRACK, INC.

Today I worked the day shift. They were short-handed, so I picked up a shift for a change of scenery.

The day shift is a different world. There are less crackheads and drunks, more schoolkids and working moms. But there is the occasional weird episode.

Around noon, I'm dispatched to pick up at the AT&T Call Center. Big place. I pull up. Honk. Out comes a clean-cut guy, well-dressed, midthirties.

Where do you want to go?

"West End Avenue with a return," he says.

Roger that.

"Can you get me there and back in thirty minutes?"

I can try.

We roll.

What do you do here at the call center?

"I'm a manager."

His destination is an area with a lot of drug activity.

You sure you want to go to West End Avenue? I ask.

"Yes, I have to meet my wife."

OK. Double checking.

We arrive at West End Avenue. He directs me to pull up in front of a known crack house. I raise an eyebrow.

The guy gets out and walks straight into the crack house. Either this is his house, or he's buying crack. He returns to the cab a few minutes later.

You good?

"I'm straight."

We roll back toward his workplace. Before I can figure out a way to politely ask what he was doing there, he lights up a pipe and begins smoking a crack rock in the back seat of the cab. Broad daylight. In traffic.

I tell him to stop.

"I'm just smoking tobacco."

It doesn't smell like tobacco, I say.

He ignores me. People are wild.

I drop him off at work. He tips me a few bucks. I watch him walk away. I now understand why my cell phone service sucks.

Crackheads are running the place.

LONG LIVE SUICIDE

It's a Tuesday night. 1:43 a.m.

"Pick up at the courthouse," says the dispatcher.

City, state, or federal? I ask.

"The guy sounds drunk," answers the dispatcher. "He didn't say."

10-4.

I drive to the city courthouse first and make a lap around the parking lot. Honk a few times. No one appears. So, I U-turn and drive to the federal courthouse. I start honking a block before I even get there, figuring the guy who called may already be passed out in a bush in the area.

HONK. HONK. HONK.

Eventually, I see movement in a park across the street. A man emerges from behind a tree and waves at me. He is carrying a duffle bag and a can of beer. He's in his late forties, skinny, with glasses. He walks up to the cab. I watch him closely. He throws his bag in the back and sits up front.

Hi.

"My name's Suicide," he says.

Nice to meet you. Where to?

"Anywhere the fuck away from here! They got cops everywhere."

OK.

We roll out.

Where are we really going? I ask.

"I'll give you directions. It's my secret spot. I can't tell anyone about it."

OK. Why?

"You cabdrivers know too many people."

Relax, I say.

"I can't relax. I got too much to do and not enough time to do it."

He gives me vague directions to the area he wants to go.

What's your story? I ask.

"I'm a tramp from Oklahoma," he says. "I've been traveling for twelve years. I like my freedom and I like my beer." He sips his beer and stares into the distance.

"I live in the woods," he says. "And I want to keep it that way."

Suicide pulls out a checkbook.

"Look. I got $1,400 in the bank. You probably wouldn't think I had that kind of money."

221

I would not have guessed it.

"That's because you judged me."

We roll on. He gives me directions. Turn here. Turn there. Go down this road. Turn left. Eventually, he points to a parking lot bordered by a warehouse and a patch of woods.

"That's where I'm getting out."

I pull in.

He pays the fare and tips me ten dollars.

I appreciate that, Suicide.

"Have a good one."

He stands there.

"Go on. Get out of here," he says. "I ain't leaving till you're gone."

I wave and pull out. He watches me drive away. When I am far enough in the distance, I look back and see him hoist his hobo bag onto his shoulder and run toward the woods.

I smile to myself.

I like that guy.

May you live long, Suicide.

COOKING WITH GAS

Pick up at a walk-in medical clinic. An old, sweet black couple appears. The wife is in a wheelchair. The husband is aging and slow. They're still taking care of one another, sticking it out to the end. I like that.

Where to?

They give an address located in the old people projects.

We roll.

When we arrive, I notice their apartment is a good distance from the parking lot. To make their trip shorter, I drive the cab onto the front lawn of the projects and park it right outside to their front porch. Now they only have a few feet to walk.

The man pats me on the shoulder.

"Now you are cooking with gas!"

YOU AIN'T SHIT

5:31 p.m. Call to pick up at a doctor's office.

I roll up.

A woman stands outside, talking on her cell phone. I ask if she is the one who called the cab. She ignores me.

OK.

I go into the doctor's office and approach the receptionist.

Who called for the cab?

The receptionist points to the woman I passed in the parking lot. I shake my head and walk out.

The woman is still talking on her cell phone. I approach her and wave to get her attention. She looks over. I point at her and then the cab. Let's roll. She huffs and walks toward the cab. She sits in the back seat and gives me her address.

While I drive, she continues talking on her phone. Her topic of the day? She was in an accident. Someone ran a red light, wrecked her car. She sustained minor injuries, but otherwise is fine. Her plan is to sue the other driver and get paid.

We roll toward her house. She finishes her conversation and claps her cell phone shut.

"Why are you driving so motherfucking fast?" she asks.

I inform her that we work on commission, which means there is no hourly wage, which means we have to rush around, grabbing as many calls as possible to make money. That's why most cabdrivers drive fast.

She doesn't like my explanation.

"Nigga, who you think you is?" she says. "Look, I love my life and I want to live my life, nigga!"

I inform her that if she is not satisfied with my driving, I can stop, and she can get out and I can call her another cab. This really sets her off.

"Nigga, come make me get out! Come get me out this motherfucking cab. I dare you, nigga!"

I pull the cab into a parking lot. Stop.

Here we are.

She stays in the cab.

"Nigga, come kick me out this cab! I'll own this bitch in a year! Come on, nigga!"

I ain't moving till you shut the fuck up, I say.

Bad move. Telling her that was a mistake, because it really sets her off even more. Now she won't shut up at all. I put the cab in gear and drive toward her destination.

"Nigga, you ain't shit! You just a broke-ass cabdriver! Don't fuck with me! I got niggas that kill your ass for two rocks!"

She rants for ten minutes. I try to ignore her.

"Get me home, nigga."

Upon arrival at her destination, she tosses her money at me.

"Nigga, you ain't shit!"

She stomps out of the cab and slams the door. As I pull away she spanks her ass and yells at me.

"Kiss my ass, nigga! You ain't shit! Kiss my motherfucking ass!"

I shake my head. Damn. She's good.

Good at what? I ask.

Good at driving a motherfucker crazy.

COKE & COCK

Call to pick up in a middle-class residential neighborhood. My passenger is a male in his early sixties. His name is Billy. He wants to go cruising for a male prostitute.

OK. Let's roll. Just tell me where to go.

"I will."

Billy is a Lafayette native. In the 1980s, he shot amphetamines. Then, he graduated to coke. He still enjoys its effects. Billy used to own a bar.

"I lost too much money," he says.

Now he is a cook on an offshore oil rig. He has two favorite things.

"I like to shoot coke and suck cock," he says. "Same time. That's my thing."

Cocaine and cock. He says he won't do one without the other. If there's coke around, he'll shoot it in his arm, but only if there is a cock available. Got to have goals.

We roll. First stop: downtown. Near a gay club.

"A lot of hustlers hang out on this corner," he says. "Most of them are addicts."

We make the block a few times, but not much is happening. There is only one guy on the street, and he is in a wheelchair.

"I wouldn't know what to do with that."

We roll on.

Second stop: Greyhound bus station. We make a few laps around the parking lot. He doesn't see any male prostitutes there. Just people waiting for their buses.

We roll on.

Billy begins to get frustrated.

"What is wrong with this town?"

I mention that it's wintertime and it's probably a tough living for a male prostitute in a cow town.

We roll on to a third location. It's a city park near the airport. There are several cars driving around the park. It's dark and poorly lit. We pass several middle-aged guys in cars who slowly drive by us. Everyone stares at the other, but nothing happens. It seems they're all looking for male prostitutes.

We see a jogger. Billy wants to talk to him. We roll up alongside the jogger. Window down.

Billy: Hey!

Jogger: Can I help you?

Billy: Yeah! What's up?

Jogger: (quizzically) Not much . . .

Billy: You want to go for a ride?

Jogger: No, thanks.

Billy: I'm looking for a party.

Jogger: No, thanks.

The jogger continues his run.

We make another lap and see more middle-aged men driving around the park in their cars. No luck. We roll out. Billy is really starting to get bummed out. He looks at me.

"I've got coke at the house," he says.

Not interested, I say. No disrespect.

We make one more pass downtown but see no male prostitutes. Even the wheelchair guy has gone home.

"Take me home."

I drop off Billy at his house, unfortunately leaving his mission unaccomplished.

THE LAZY MAN

Midnight. I get a call to pick up at a trailer park. I pull up. Honk. Out comes a guy in his late twenties with his two-year-old son. They climb in. Immediately the stench of a dirty diaper hits me. I'll refer to the dad as Lumpy.

Where are we going?

He gives me an address. It's an apartment complex on the other side of town where Lumpy's baby momma lives.

"We got to drop off my kid."

Yep.

We roll.

Lumpy makes meaningless conversation. He reveals himself to be a moron. I ask what kind of work he does.

"I can't work right now. I got a case."

A case of what?

"I was in a car accident. I'm filing a personal injury lawsuit."

Oh.

"Waiting on that money."

We arrive at the apartment complex. I ask Lumpy what number is her apartment?

"I don't know the number. But I know where it's at."

Unbelievable. With some trial and error, we locate her apartment building. Lumpy gets out. He leaves the kid in the car with me. I shake my head. Lumpy approaches a door and knocks on it.

No answer.

Lumpy knocks again. Then, he walks around in circles and makes a call on his cell phone. He walks back to the cab.

"She ain't here."

What do you want to do?

"I guess bring me back."

Do you have money to pay the cab fare both ways?

"No. She was going to pay the fare."

Roll my eyes. What a mess this dude is. Now I have to drive them both back and pay their fare. Thirty-one dollars, round trip. Fuck it.

Lumpy shrugs his shoulders.

"What do you want me to do?"

I want you to handle your business like a fucking man.

He shrugs again.

I dislike this guy and I don't even know him. I look at Lumpy and his kid. They're both pitiful. I put the cab in gear and drive them back to Lumpy's trailer.

SLAVE NATION

Call to pick up at a trailer park in Henderson, Louisiana.

"Sounds like a Mexican, going to the Greyhound station," says the dispatcher.

10-4.

I roll to Henderson. It's a twenty-two-minute drive. When I arrive, I have trouble locating the trailer park. It's not listed on any maps. I stop at a gas station and ask the clerk if he knows where it is.

"You looking for them foreigners?"

Yeah, I guess so.

"There's a whole bunch of them living up the road in some trailers," he says.

He gives me directions.

"They all work at the McDonald's across the street."

Duly noted. Thanks.

I roll out and locate the trailer park right where he said it would be. It's a run-down, depressing place. Twenty trailers sitting in an open field. I locate the customer's trailer, #16. I pull up, honk, and wait.

A few dudes loiter around outside. Bent bicycles are scattered about the yard. While I'm waiting, I remember reading an article in the local news a few weeks ago. Apparently, McDonald's is importing people from other countries to work in their restaurants. I guess there's a shortage of Americans who want to work at McDonald's.

I honk again.

Finally, a guy pokes his head out of the door and waves at me. Five minutes pass. No one comes out. I hop out of the cab, walk to the door, and knock.

No answer.

Fuck it. I turn the knob and poke my head in the door.

Hello! Did someone call a cab?

No one replies.

I see sleeping bags on the floor. Dirty carpet. Spent candy wrappers. An Xbox. But there is no one in sight. I walk in and announce my presence.

Hello! Anybody here?

No answer.

As I stand there, a pale, middle-aged woman walks through the door behind me. She looks at me confused.

"Who are you?"

She speaks with an eastern European accent.

Cab driver, I say. Someone called a cab.

"Did someone call you from here?"

Yes, I think so. And who are you?

"I am their supervisor."

OK. At McDonald's?

"Yes."

She walks around me and goes down the hall. She knocks on a bedroom door. A man's voice in the room answers her. He, too, has a foreign accent.

"Can you come out here?" she asks. "Luis, come out here! You are supposed to be at work!"

"I no come out!" he says.

"You are supposed to be at work!" she yells at the closed bedroom door.

"No! I no like job!" he says.

It looks as if I've stumbled into some kind of slave labor camp for fast food workers. I'm guessing this is the guy that called the cab. Maybe he is trying to escape.

"Go away!" he says. "I no work."

"Luis, you need to come to work, now!"

"I NO WORK ANYMORE!"

She frustratedly huffs, walks around me, and exits the trailer. I hear her outside, talking to someone on her cell phone. Weird scene. I'm losing faith in this call.

I knock on the bedroom door and try talking to the dude.

Hey, man. I'm your cab driver. I'm going to help you get out of here, I explain.

"I no come out!" he yells back at me.

I tell him it's OK. I'm here to help you.

"No, you not. You take me to work!"

No, buddy. I'm here to take you to the bus station.

I try the doorknob. It is locked. I bang on the door.

Come on, buddy. Let's get out of here. I'm not here to bring you to work.

"I no come out!"

A Hispanic guy suddenly darts out of a closet in the hallway and runs out of the trailer.

What kind of kooky place is this?

I knock on the door again.

I'm here to help, man, I tell him again. Let's go.

Silence, then: "I no go!"

OK. Fair enough. I can't make this guy leave. I can't even get him to open the door. It's a wasted trip. I guess he's going to stay here at the McDonald's slave ship.

Who are all these people? What the fuck is going on? And most importantly, what the fuck am I doing here? I mean, I know I'm doing my job. But in the bigger picture, what the fuck am I doing? I'm standing in a trashed-out trailer park, surrounded by poor people from other countries, working at jobs they hate, which in turn makes me realize I am starting to hate my own job. I'm one of them! Maybe I no longer have the heart and soul to do this cabdriving shit.

I'm burnt out.

I've been driving a cab for five years. It's been an incredible journey, but also heartbreaking and sad. It might be time to move on. I've become desensitized to the violence, the drug addicts, the drunks, and the poor, broken people. I think I've seen too much weirdness and pain on this job. Too much poverty and struggle.

I sigh and walk out of the trailer. I walk down the steps, past the dead bicycles, past the heaps of trash, past the strange lady on her cell phone, and past the listless dudes still hanging around outside. I walk past it all and climb into the cab.

I drive it back into the streets as the sun sets upon the ghetto.

Like a lot of the calls in the cab, this one turned into something I wasn't expecting. It went from a call from a dude trying to escape his job and life here to *my* escape. I realize my journey in the cab has come to an end.

It's time.

This will be my last shift.

I blow past it all.

A grand procession of names, faces, and addresses rattles through my mind like dirty ghosts coiled in the ivy of my notebook. I stomp on the accelerator and speed down the highway, wind blasting through the interior. My eyes watering with the cider of tears.

I've become so jaded at this job, dealing with so many dysfunctional people.

The fuck ups.

The crackheads.

The drunks.

The drug dealers.

The prostitutes.

The knuckleheads.

The thieves.

It's not their fault.
It's not mine either.
But I'm tired of dealing with them.
I'm emotionally exhausted.
And my own inadequate reactions to them
   Have sometimes made me dislike the nature of my own soul.
I feel as if I've failed some kind of spiritual test.
I now understand something I didn't realize five years ago when I started
this job.
   It is easier
   To be a Buddha on the mountain
   Than a saint in the streets.

And with that, I plow through the night
   And on to the next chapter in my life
   However heartbreaking
   Challenging
   Maddening
   Surreal
   Exultant
   Or joyous
It may reveal itself to be.

ABOUT THE AUTHOR

Dege Legg is a Grammy-nominated musician (*Django Unchained* original soundtrack) and award-winning writer born and raised in southern Louisiana. In addition to driving a cab, he has a BA in philosophy and has worked as a dishwasher, journalist, manual laborer, warehouseman, mechanic, driver, line cook, and a caseworker in a homeless shelter in order to support his artistic compulsions. He writes music, records, and tours the USA and Europe with his band Brother Dege & The Brethren. Visit him at brotherdege.net.

photo by Lucius A. Fontenot